VOLUME 1

Miss Brenda's
BEDTIME STORIES

This book is lovingly presented to

_____

By: _____

On this special occasion

_____

Date: _____

VOLUME 1

Miss Brenda's
BEDTIME STORIES

BRENDA WALSH

Based on
True Character-Building Stories
for the Whole Family!

3ABN BOOKS

Three Angels Broadcasting Network
P.O. Box 220, West Frankfort, Illinois
www.3ABN.org

Pacific Press® Publishing Association
Nampa, Idaho
Oshawa, Ontario, Canada
www.pacificpress.com

Design/Layout: Chrystique Neibauer "CQ" | cqgraphicdesign.com
Cover Photography: David B. Sherwin
Project Coordinator: Mellisa Hoffman | finaleditservices.com

Copyright © 2011 by Brenda Walsh
Printed in the United States of America
All rights reserved

The author assumes full responsibility for the accuracy of all facts and quotations as cited in this book.

Additional copies of this book are available from two locations:

Adventist Book Centers®: Call toll-free 1-800-765-6955 or visit http://www.adventistbookcenter.com.

3ABN: Call (618) 627-4651 or visit http://www.store.3abn.org.

3ABN Books is dedicated to bringing you the best in published materials consistent with the mission of Three Angels Broadcasting Network. Our goal is to uplift Jesus Christ through books, audio, and video materials by our family of 3ABN presenters. Our in-depth Bible study guides, devotionals, biographies, and lifestyle materials promote whole person health and the mending of broken people. For more information, call 618-627-4651 or visit 3ABN's Web site: www.3ABN.org.

Scripture quotations marked NIV are from the HOLY BIBLE, NEW INTERNATIONAL VERSION®. Copyright © 1973, 1978, 1984 by International Bible Society. Used by permission of Zondervan Publishing House. All rights reserved.

Scriptures quoted from NKJV are from The New King James Version, copyright © 1979, 1980, 1982, Thomas Nelson, Inc., Publishers.

Scripture quotations marked NLT are taken from the Holy Bible, New Living Translation, copyright © 1996, 2004, 2007. Used by permission by Tyndale House Publishers, Inc., Wheaton, Illinois 60189. All rights reserved.

Scripture quotations marked KJV are from the King James Version of the Bible.

Library of Congress Cataloging-in-Publication Data:

Walsh, Brenda, 1953-
Miss Brenda's bedtime stories : true character building stories for the whole family! / Brenda Walsh.
    p. cm.
ISBN 13: 978-0-8163-2409-5 (hard cover)
ISBN 10: 0-8163-2409-3 (hard cover)
1. Christian children—Religious life—Anecdotes. 2. Families—Religious life—Anecdotes. I. Title. II. Title: Bedtime stories.
BV4571.3.W35 2011
249—dc22

                                                             2011007590

11 12 13 14 15 • 5 4 3 2 1

DEDICATION

Miss Brenda with her grandsons

◀ **Dear Michael,** you are one of God's greatest blessings to me. There is nothing I enjoy more than spending time with you! I love it that you trust me enough to talk to me about anything and everything. Most of all it brings joy to my heart to see how much you love to talk to Jesus.

I love wrestling with you and your brother, playing fun games, or building Legos, but I especially love tucking you in at night, singing to you, and listening to your prayers. Always remember that our real home is in heaven with Jesus. With heartfelt love, I dedicate this book to you. I love you!

—Grandma

◀ **Dear Jason,** you have filled my life with so much joy and happiness and I treasure every moment that I can spend with you. I love the times that we snuggle up on the sofa and read stories together and talk about all the fun we'll have in heaven. Some day soon, Jesus is coming to take us home with Him and then we will always be together. I'm excited that I won't have to fly on an airplane to spend time with you because we'll have mansions right next door to each other! I am dedicating this book to you so that you will always know how very much Jesus and I love you.

—Grandma

ACKNOWLEDGMENTS

With Special Thanks

Dr. Kay Kuzma

I want to thank Dr. Kay Kuzma for all her hours and hours spent editing *Miss Brenda's Bedtime Stories*. She is one of the most generous, kind, and talented people I know and these stories would not have been the same without her! I admire and respect her professionalism, creative writing skills, and her loving service for others. Her love for our Lord and Savior shines through in all she does. She has blessed my life in so many ways and I thank God for the gift of her friendship.

Brenda Walsh

Author Appreciation

I want to personally thank each of these best-selling authors for their generous contribution of stories. It is truly an honor and privilege to include them in *Miss Brenda's Bedtime Stories*. Each author was personally selected to be a part of this five book series because of their creative and professional writing style, incredible talent, and love for Jesus! To each of them I extend my sincere and heartfelt thanks!

Jean Boonstra   Karen Collum   David Edgren   Kay Kuzma   Charles Mills

Seth Pierce   Kay D. Rizzo   Kimberley Tagert-Paul   Jerry D. Thomas

ACKNOWLEDGMENTS

With Heartfelt Thanks To . . .

MY STORY AND PHOTO TEAM: **Battle Creek Academy** for opening your doors for the cover photo shoot. **Ted and Bonnie Bloomfield** for the many hours spent developing the Excel spreadsheet. **Dr. Buddy and Tina Houghtaling** for organizing and planning the cover photo shoot. **Larry McLucas** for your friendship, posing for photos, and support of the Kids' Time ministry. **Dick and Lucy Neuharth** for photos, for sewing two very special purses, and your treasured friendship! **Mike Neuharth** and **Madison Allen** for being "minute men" and posing for a photo. **Kim Otis** for answering a Facebook plea and photographing your cat. **Dan Hansen** for *brainstorming* story titles! **Mellisa Hoffman** for your project coordination, organizational skills, being the "spelling champ," tenacity to *getting the job done*, and your loyalty and friendship! **Hannah and Lance Hoffman** for your patience during all the long hours your mom spent working on the book project. **Chrystique Neibauer** for the incredible layout and graphic design of the entire project, for extra long hours, patience, and being a friend I can count on! **Dave Sherwin** for volunteering your time to photograph each cover. **Ina Stanaland** for writing endless e-mails and reading and categorizing all the stories.

MY MINISTRY SUPPORT TEAM: **Carole Derry-Bretsch** for e-mailing your numerous friends to find the perfect photos and, most of all, for being my lifelong friend! **Peg O'Brien Bernhard** for always being there for me, listening, believing in me, and for your love and friendship! **Kari Avery-Duffy** for hours spent researching stories, answering letters, and your dedication to the Kids' Time ministries. **Marie Macri** for being a precious friend—always there for me. I love you dearly! **Rita Showers** for a lifetime of memories, friendship, and the best neighbor a girl could have! **Nancy Sterling** for mentoring me, looking out for my best interests, and for your loving friendship!

MY FAMILY: My precious husband, **Tim Walsh,** for never complaining about the time I spent working on this project, for your constant support, help, and patience, but most of all, for your unconditional love you give me every day! **Rebecca Lynn and Linda Kay** for your love and support and allowing me to share your stories. My parents, **James and Bernice Micheff,** for your prayers, letting my team take over your house, for endless hours finding photos, and for all those great meals! To my **sisters, brothers, grandsons, aunts, uncles, nieces, and nephews,** for your patience and loving understanding concerning the many hours I spent working on this project, even though you would have preferred I was spending time with you! I am so very grateful for my precious family and love you with all my heart!

Those who shared their stories with me:

Melody Shelton Firestone	Donna Shelly
Kristin Hutchinson	Danny Shelton
Kevin & Angela Kuzma	Michael Ulrich
Shirley Marsh	Linda Kay Walsh
Christine Haines Regester	Karlie Zabarowski

ABOUT "MISS BRENDA"

Miss Brenda & Maxwell

Brenda Walsh is a vivacious, loving, and generous Christian with a heart for ministry and a burning desire to share the love and joy of Jesus. When she started praying, "Lord, use me in a special way," God did! And the resulting, amazing miracle stories have been an inspiration to thousands across the world who have heard her dynamic presentations or read her attention-grabbing books. Her message is one of encouragement and hope to those who want to be used by God. Hearing Brenda is truly a life-changing experience, whether it's at a women's ministries retreat, a prayer conference, a church-based weekend event, or a children's ministries seminar.

Brenda is best known as "Miss Brenda," the producer and host of **Kids' Time**, a popular daily children's program on Three Angels Broadcasting Network (3ABN). She is also a frequent guest on the *3ABN Today* program, cooking and singing with her sisters, Linda and Cinda. Together they have authored vegan vegetarian cookbooks and recorded several gospel CDs. Brenda also has her own solo CD, **My Wonderful Lord**.

Brenda is the author of **Battered to Blessed**, her life story of being a victim of domestic violence; and **Passionate Prayer**, which features her own personal stories of answered prayer. She has also co-authored several books with her friend Kay Kuzma. This is her first of five volumes of **Miss Brenda's Bedtime Stories**.

Miss Brenda & children on the *Kids' Time* set.

In addition to ministering to others, Brenda is a registered nurse, interior decorator, and floral designer. Brenda is married to Tim Walsh, has two grown daughters, Becky and Linda Kay, and two grandsons, Michael James and Jason Patrick.

www.kidstime4jesus.org

LESSON INDEX

Accepting Differences
Brave Kwame – 45

Attitude Change
Mean Old Rooster – 132
The Unmailed Letter – 56

Bravery
Brave Kwame – 45
Trapped in Wildcat Cave – 149

Cheating, Results of
Almost Perfect Picture – 78
The Spelling Champion – 69

Disobedience, Results of
A Squirrel's Tale – 15
Devil's Tongue Temptation – 122
Tackle-Tag Disaster – 50
The Forbidden Concert – 111

Fear
Snakes Alive – 89

Friendship
Brave Kwame – 45
Forgotten Lunch – 117
Guilty by Association – 137
The Unmailed Letter – 56

Forgiveness
The Unmailed Letter – 56

Friends, Choosing
Guilty by Association – 137

Giving
Living Like Tahili – 84

God's Protection
Help! Save Me! – 106

Honesty
Girl Who Cried "Deer" – 127
Green Apple Gum – 25

Kindness
The Unmailed Letter – 56

Prayer, Answers to
Fat Cat Freddie – 40
Forgotten Lunch – 117
Help! Save Me! – 106
Maxwell, the *Kids' Time* Dog – 62
Tracy's Terrifying Jump – 21
Prayed for Purse – 29
Snakes Alive – 89
Washed Away – 156

Pride, Results of
Devil's Tongue Temptation – 122
Ice Queen – 94
The Spelling Champion – 69

Responsibility
Kristin's New Shoes – 143

Self-Sacrifice
Living Like Tahili – 84

Serving Others
Living Like Tahili – 84
Trapped in Wildcat Cave – 149

Thankfulness
Intruder in the Chimney – 100
The Unwanted Train – 74

TABLE OF CONTENTS

- Introduction 13
- A Squirrel's Tale 15
- Tracy's Terrifying Jump 21
- Green Apple Gum 25
- Prayed for Purse 29
- Zack's Secret 35
- Fat Cat Freddie 40
- Brave Kwame 45
- Tackle-Tag Disaster 50
- The Unmailed Letter 56
- Maxwell, the *Kids' Time* Dog 62
- The Spelling Champion 69
- The Unwanted Train 74
- Almost Perfect Picture 78
- Living Like Tahili 84
- Snakes Alive 89
- Ice Queen 94
- Intruder in the Chimney 100
- Help! Save Me! 106
- The Forbidden Concert 111
- Forgotten Lunch 117
- Devil's Tongue Temptation 122
- Girl Who Cried "Deer" 127
- Mean Old Rooster 132
- Guilty by Association 137
- Kristin's New Shoes 143
- Trapped in Wildcat Cave 149
- Washed Away 156

INTRODUCTION

Stories have power to touch us and change us. They can help us understand what another person is feeling and help us see things from a new perspective. They can help us understand "Why?" and see the reasoning behind "Be careful!" They can help us learn lessons without having to suffer from making mistakes! That's why Jesus taught by telling stories. He knew that stories help us understand.

This book is full of stories told for the same reasons. So much effort, love, and prayer have gone into collecting and preparing *Miss Brenda's Bedtime Stories*! Based on true stories contributed from people around the world, each story has been written especially for Miss Brenda by beloved and best-selling authors (and some written by Miss Brenda herself!). They are sure to be loved by children and treasured by parents and grandparents and all who read them.

Brenda has shared these stories to help kids everywhere develop strong characters, understand important lessons, and most important, learn to be good friends of Jesus. These pages are full of stories that are heart-touching, soul-searching, fun-filled, adventurous, and meant to be shared!

May these stories bring laughter to the eyes, wisdom to the mind, and understanding to the heart of everyone who hears them. And may there be a double blessing of peace and joy to each grown-up who takes a few precious moments to share them with a child.

Be sure to collect all five volumes of
Miss Brenda's Bedtime Stories!

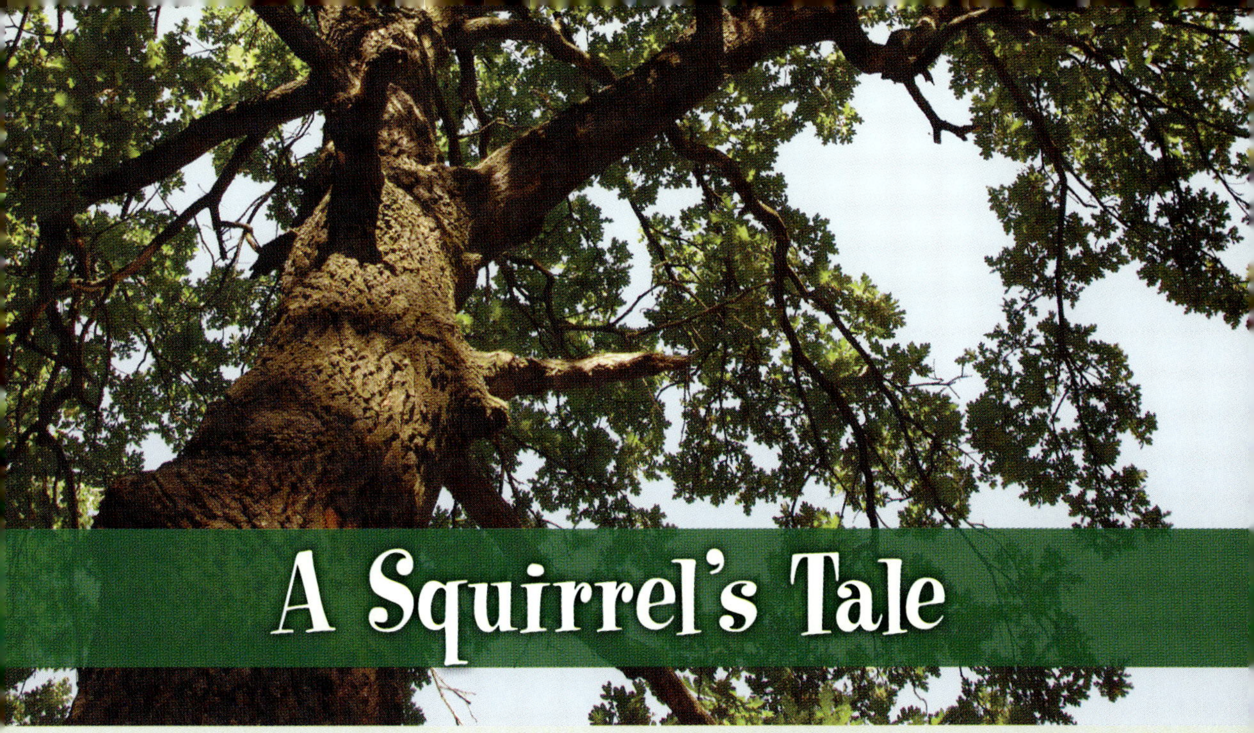

A Squirrel's Tale

High up in the tallest branches of the giant oak tree that grew in Rusty's backyard lived a family of fluffy gray squirrels. Each evening, right before supper, Rusty and his father would watch the furry creatures scurry up and down the trunk of the tree collecting the walnuts Dad had placed on the ground.

"I bet I could train one of those squirrels to take a nut from my hand," Rusty bragged to his dad. "Maybe if he got used to me, he'd even let me pet him."

"That wouldn't be a very good idea, son," Dad explained. "As friendly as squirrels seem to be, they are still wild animals and could bite you, especially if they were frightened. And if they happened to be sick, they could give you a bad disease. Then we'd have to take you to the hospital for shots, and you know how you hate shots."

"But I wouldn't scare them. I'd stay very still," Rusty insisted.

A Squirrel's Tale

"No, son. Leave the squirrels alone. Don't feed them without me." Dad tossed the last of the walnuts toward the tree. "Time to go inside for supper. Mom's making homemade pizza tonight."

At the mention of his favorite meal, Rusty's stomach growled. "Yum! I'm sure hungry. How about you, Dad?"

"You bet!"

"Race you to the back door!" Rusty shouted as he took off running. He thundered onto the back porch and slammed against the screen door. "Beat ya!" Rusty laughed.

"Not by much." Huffing and puffing, Dad charged onto the porch. "But you had a head start!"

"Fair and square, Dad," Rusty laughed, " 'cause you have longer legs."

Rusty opened the screen door and bounded into the kitchen. "*Umm*, the pizza smells yummy."

"Not as good as my favorite cherry pie," Dad exclaimed as he kissed Mom on the cheek. "You've been busy this afternoon."

She laughed and playfully swatted Dad with the dishtowel. "Go on now. Hurry and wash up. The pizza just came out of the oven."

All evening Rusty could think of nothing else but the squirrels. Oh, how fun it would be to train at least one of them to eat from his hand. The more he thought about it, the more determined he became to try. As he lay on his bed in the dark, he developed a plan he knew would work.

The next morning, after Dad left for the office, Mom was sorting the dirty clothes that needed washing, when Rusty sauntered into the laundry

A Squirrel's Tale

room and casually asked his mother if he could feed the squirrels. Busy scrubbing grass stains off of Rusty's pants, Mom only half heard his question. "Sure, honey. Be careful."

"Thanks, Mom!" Rusty ran from the laundry room before Mom could change her mind. In the kitchen, he opened the freezer door and removed the bag of walnuts from the freezer. He opened the bag and scooped out a handful and stuffed them into his pockets. After putting the bag back in the freezer, Rusty looked down the hall to make sure Mom wasn't watching, and then quickly ran outside. The screen door slammed behind him, sending the gray squirrels scurrying up the trunk of the tree.

Rusty felt a thrill of anticipation as he made a trail of nuts from the trunk of the tree to the house and then waited on the porch steps for the squirrels to come to him. And come they did! One at a time, they darted for the nuts, coming closer and closer to where Rusty sat. To his delight, the littlest squirrel, his favorite, was also the bravest. To retrieve the last few walnuts, the tiniest squirrel inched closer and closer. Barely daring to breathe, Rusty held the last walnut between his fingers. *Would the squirrel take it?*

The squirrel stopped less than six inches from Rusty's hand. The animal glanced first in one direction and then the other. He looked at the nut and then the boy. Without taking his eyes off Rusty, the squirrel inched closer and closer. Just as the squirrel extended his neck to take the nut out of Rusty's fingers, a noisy motorcycle went by, popping its engine. Frightened by the loud noise, the squirrel nipped the end of Rusty's finger with his sharp teeth as he grabbed the nut, then fled across the yard and up the tree.

A Squirrel's Tale

"Ouch!" Rusty screamed and ran inside the house, crying and holding his finger.

"What happened?" Mom asked. "Are you OK?"

Suddenly, Rusty remembered Dad's warning about having to go to the doctor to get shots if a squirrel bit him. He also remembered that Dad had said to leave the squirrels alone. "I . . . I . . . I . . . jabbed myself with a sharp stick," Rusty sobbed.

Mom held his finger and studied the wound carefully. "The skin is broken and it's bleeding just a little. I'll wash it off, put on some anti-bacterial cream and a Band-Aid, and you'll be fine."

Rusty's finger throbbed with pain throughout the afternoon, but he didn't tell his mother. When his father came home from work, he wasn't feeling any better. "Hey, what about going out and feeding the squirrels while Mom finishes supper?"

Rusty hung his head, "Naw, I don't feel like it today."

"He hasn't been feeling well since he cut his finger on a stick this morning," Mom called from the kitchen.

Dad glanced at his son and then at Rusty's bandaged finger. "Let me take a look."

"Oh, it's not too bad," Rusty mumbled. Deep down inside, Rusty began to feel very uncomfortable.

Dad ignored Rusty's protests and proceeded to remove the Band-Aid. He studied the injury for several seconds. The tip of Rusty's finger was fiery red and swollen. "Are you sure you injured your finger with a stick?"

Rusty's face paled. "Uh, um, uh, yeah."

Dad looked straight into his son's eyes and asked, "Rusty, this is important. Tell me the truth. Were you feeding the squirrels and one of

A Squirrel's Tale

them bit you? If so, I need to know now!"

Rusty glanced down at the floor and then nervously toward the kitchen, not wanting his mother to hear. "Yeah, but I asked Mom's permission first," he countered.

Dad's voice sounded serious, "Didn't I tell you to leave the squirrels alone? Didn't I say they could bite you and possibly give you some awful disease?"

Rusty's lower lip quivered. "B-B-But Dad, my plan was working. If that noisy motorcycle hadn't gone by and scared the squirrel, he would have eaten out of my hand instead of biting me."

Dad looked at his son sternly. Rusty knew he was in for a serious talking-to. "Son, even a perfect plan wouldn't have made this right. First, you disobeyed me. Second, you took advantage of your mother. She didn't know that I told you not to feed the squirrels without me. And third, you lied to Mom and me. Those lies could have cost you your life. One of the diseases squirrels carry is lockjaw. People can get it if bitten by an infected animal. Unless this disease is treated immediately, it could kill you."

"I'm so sorry," sniffed Rusty. "Am I going to die?"

"No, you're not going to die because Mom and I are going to take you right now to the hospital for a shot. Supper will have to wait."

During the ride to the hospital, tears slid down Rusty's cheeks as he stared at his swollen finger. He didn't want to die, but he certainly wasn't looking forward to getting a shot.

At the hospital parking lot, Dad found a place to park the car while Mom put her arm around Rusty and led him into the crowded emergency room. He found a seat while Mom explained to a nurse what had happened. After what seemed like forever, the nurse led Rusty into a curtained cubical. "Hop on to the table," she said. "The doctor will be here in a few minutes."

After the doctor examined him, a nurse came in with what looked to Rusty like the largest needle in the world. Rusty squeezed his eyes shut and braced for the pain he knew would come. "Ouch, that hurts!" he

A Squirrel's Tale

cried. Oh, how he wished he hadn't disobeyed his dad.

On the way home from the hospital, Dad stopped at a local taco place for a quick supper. Rusty nibbled on his bean burrito. He didn't feel much like eating. He looked across the booth at his parents. "Mom, Dad, I'm so sorry. Please forgive me?"

"Of course we forgive you," Mom replied.

"And will Jesus forgive me too?"

"Yes, He will," Dad said. "Jesus promises that when we ask for forgiveness He is faithful and just to forgive our sins."

"Even the really bad ones?"

"Of course," Mom said. "And do you know what He does next?"

Rusty shook his head.

"Jesus dumps them in the deepest spot in the ocean, and they are never, ever to be seen again!"

"I want Jesus to do that for me. Can we pray right here?"

Rusty reached across the booth and took hold of his parents' hands and bowed his head, "Dear Jesus, please forgive me for disobeying my dad and for lying to my parents. Thank You, Jesus, for forgiving me. Please take those nasty old lies and dump them in the ocean right now. Amen!"

In a few weeks, Rusty's finger was completely healed; but every time he looked at the scar, he thanked Jesus for throwing his sins in the deepest part of the sea. ∎

> *If we confess our sins, he . . . will forgive us our sins and purify us from all unrighteousness.*
> —1 John 1:9, NIV

Tracy's Terrifying Jump

"**W**atch this!" Todd yelled over the sound of the boat's loud roar. Tracy watched her older brother as he flew up into the air with his skis and jumped over the boat's wake. Tracy loved to watch her big brother water ski. She loved being with her family at the lake. There was only one problem. Tracy didn't know how to swim yet.

"Nice jump!" Tracy's other brother, Trevor, shouted over his shoulder to Todd. "Doesn't that look like fun?" he said to Tracy. Trevor liked to drive the boat while Todd skied, then they would switch places. He tugged on Tracy's blue life jacket. "When are you going to ski with us?"

"Oh please, Trevor, can I go skiing today?"

Trevor laughed. "As soon as you learn how to swim, you can go skiing." He pulled his hands up to his mouth and shouted, "Todd! It's my turn!"

Before long, the boys headed back to the dock. "I hope Mom already has lunch ready—I'm starving!" Todd said

Tracy's Terrifying Jump

as he shut off the engine. "Trevor, you tie us up. Come on, Tracy. I'll race you to the house."

Tracy knew that Todd was only pretending to run slowly so she could win, but he looked so funny that she laughed anyway. They all dropped their life jackets on the porch and went inside. As the screen door shut behind them, her brothers headed into the kitchen, but Tracy stopped and stared out at the water. *If I learned to swim today, I could ski too,* she thought. *And that would surprise everyone!*

She slipped quietly out the door and headed back to the dock. First, she sat on the edge and swished her feet in the water. *Swimming isn't hard,* Tracy said to herself. She'd been watching her brothers swim all summer. *Even fish can do it, and I'm a lot bigger than they are. And I know how to hold my breath. I do it all the time in the bathtub.*

Then Tracy stood up—and jumped into the water.

Trevor heard the water splash through the kitchen window. "Wow! That must have been a big fish! Did you hear it, Tracy? Tracy?"

Tracy sank down until her toes were touching the sand at the bottom of the lake. It wasn't really very deep there, but it was deep enough that the water was over her head. Tracy immediately began thrashing her arms and legs, trying to remember what her brothers looked like when they were swimming, but it wasn't working. She didn't seem to be getting anywhere at all! The more she kicked and squirmed, the more she seemed to sink until her feet touched the bottom again! *Oh Jesus, please help me. I'm drowning!* Kicking with all her might, she managed to get her head above water, and gulped a big breath of air. Then down she sank again.

Trevor looked out the screen door. "Her life jacket is there so Tracy can't

Tracy's Terrifying Jump

be—wait a minute! Todd! Quick, get Mom and Dad! I think Tracy jumped in the lake!" he shouted as he raced out the door.

Tracy was still at the bottom of the lake. She could see the boat up above her. *Oh, how am I going to get to the top! Am I going to die?* She wanted to scream. *Jesus save me,* she prayed.

Tracy was now terrified and beginning to panic. She didn't know how much longer she could hold her breath and no matter how much she kicked her arms and legs, she wasn't able to get to the top again.

Trevor ran out onto the dock, shouting, "Tracy, where are you?" He stared down, trying to see Tracy in the water. But he wasn't just staring. He was praying. "Oh, Jesus, please help me find Tracy. Don't let her drown. Help me find my sister." He was still praying as he jumped into the water.

By now, Todd and Mom and Dad were racing down to the dock, shouting for Tracy and Trevor.

Tracy could hear them shouting, but it sounded very far away. She flapped her arms harder, but got nowhere. Just when she thought she couldn't wait a second longer for air, she heard a loud splash and Trevor was right there beside her. He grabbed her quickly, and they shot up to the surface of the water.

Tracy gasped and took a great big breath as Todd's arms reached down and pulled her up to the dock. Trevor popped up right beside them. Her mom and dad were so relieved to see their precious little girl. "Honey, you scared us so much!" they cried while they hugged her. "Why did you jump in the water all by yourself? And without your life jacket?"

"I just wanted to surprise everyone by learning to swim," Tracy explained, shivering more from fright than cold. "I wanted to go skiing with Trevor and Todd this afternoon."

Tracy's Terrifying Jump

Mom knelt down and wrapped a towel around her.

Trevor just stared at her. "Tracy, I didn't mean that you could ski with us today! It takes a long time to learn to swim and be safe in the water." Dad put his arm around her, and the thankful family started back toward the house. "Maybe this afternoon Todd and I will start teaching you how to swim. And the first lesson is—don't go swimming alone!" Trevor said emphatically.

While they ate lunch, Tracy told them about the fish she saw underwater. "And you should see how funny the boat looks from underneath!" she said.

Trevor shook his head. "I think your guardian angel was watching over you because I jumped in at the perfect spot, right beside you in the water!"

Tracy smiled as she took another bite of her sandwich. "I prayed for Jesus to save me and He did! He sent my brothers to help me! He must love me an awful lot!"

> *The Lord will keep you from all harm—*
> *he will watch over your life.*
> *—Psalm 121:7, NIV*

Green Apple Gum

Marcus closed his eyes, tipped up his nose, and took a long sniff. *Sniff, sniff.* "Oh, there it is. I can smell it. The best smell in the whole world—green apple flavored gum."

"Oh, I love that flavor!" his friend Zeayon said. "Where is it? How can you smell just one flavor of gum in this whole big aisle of candy and stuff?"

"I can smell it," Marcus said. "It's right down there, near the bottom in the bright green package. Green apple gum is my favorite flavor and I can smell it anywhere."

Zeayon bent over, picked up a pack of gum, and looked at the package. "That's it all right. Are you going to buy some?"

"No, I don't have any money. I don't get my allowance until tomorrow, and Mom says I have to spend my own money on gum." Marcus picked up a pack and sniffed again. "It does smell good, though."

Green Apple Gum

"Well, I'm getting two packs," Zeayon decided. "See you later!" He checked out with his mom and stopped to wave at Marcus as the winter wind whistled in through the store's open door.

"OK, bye, just shut the door on that cold air," Marcus said as he shoved his hands deeper into his coat pocket. *Hey, what's that?* he thought when his right hand touched a small piece of paper. *Did someone leave a note in my pocket?*

He pulled the paper out. *A dollar? Who put a dollar in my coat pocket?* He thought about the last time he wore his coat. *I haven't had it on since last weekend. We didn't go to the store or anything. Just to church.*

Wait! Marcus thought. *I remember! Mom gave me a dollar to put into the offering at church last week. I must have forgotten. I'll just put it in this week. Mom will understand when I tell her about it.*

At school the next day, Zeayon pulled out his two packs of gum. "It tastes just as good as it smells, Marcus!"

Marcus smelled the gum and felt the dollar that was still in his coat pocket. "I'll buy one of them from you," he said suddenly. "Here's a dollar," as he took the gum from his friend.

Zeayon looked at him. "I thought you didn't get your allowance yet."

Marcus shrugged. "My mom gave it to me early." *It's not really a lie,* he thought to himself. *She did give it to me — last week at church.* Then he started chewing his gum and stopped thinking about it.

When Mom picked him up after school, she sniffed the air. "What's that smell?" she asked.

"That's my green apple gum," Marcus said proudly.

"Where did you get green apple gum during school?" his mother wanted to know.

"Zeayon had a big pack and he—" Marcus stopped. He almost told his

 MISS BRENDA'S BEDTIME STORIES — VOLUME 1

Green Apple Gum

mother that he bought Zeayon's pack of gum. But he couldn't.

Just last night, he thought, *Mom knew I didn't have any money. She'll ask, "Where did you get money for gum?" How can I answer without telling her about the offering dollar?*

"Zeayon shared some with me," Marcus finished his sentence. *It's not really a lie,* he thought. *Zeayon did share his gum. I just had to pay for it.*

But Marcus heard another question in his mind: *If there's nothing wrong with it, then why didn't you just tell your mother about the dollar? Why did you lie to her and to Zeayon?* Suddenly, Zeayon's green apple gum didn't taste so good.

But Marcus didn't think about it again until he was sitting in church that weekend. "Now it's time for the offering," the pastor said. All at once, Marcus looked up. "Oh, no!" he said out loud.

His mom smiled. "I know you spent all of your allowance at the bookstore yesterday. Here's a dollar to put in the offering."

Marcus just stared at the dollar bill she dropped in his hand. *I spent all my allowance. Now I can't pay back the offering dollar that I spent.* He felt so bad that he could hardly even look at his mom or the pastor or anyone else.

Mom knew that something was bothering him. "What is it, Marcus?" she asked when they got home. "What's wrong?"

It only took a moment for Marcus to tell her the whole story. "I'm sorry, Mom. Can you forgive me? I didn't mean to keep the dollar or lie about it, but that gum smelled so good. And I did plan to pay it back this week. But now I can't."

His mom gave him a gentle hug. "Yes, of course I forgive you, and

Green Apple Gum

I'm sure we can find a way for you to earn that dollar and put it in the offering next week. I'm just glad you learned that when you steal or tell a lie, it doesn't just hurt the other person—it hurts you as well. I'm also glad you asked me to forgive you. Don't forget to ask Jesus to forgive you too."

Marcus finally felt like smiling again. "I already did! You know something, Mom? As much as I like green apple gum, I like how I feel when I'm honest, even better!"

> *I have shown you in every way, by laboring like this, that you must support the weak. And remember the words of the Lord Jesus, that He said, "It is more blessed to give than to receive."*
> —Acts 20:35, NKJV

Prayed for Purse

Karlie studied the wall calendar by the kitchen door. "Mom!" She whirled about, her eyes sparkling with anticipation. "Today is June first! Grandma Esther is coming!"

"Yes, that's right. We're picking her up at the airport tonight." Karlie's mother laughed as her daughter jumped up and down with excitement.

"Oh!" Karlie gasped, "I need to straighten my room before she gets here. I wouldn't want her to have to see a messy room." And away she ran.

Karlie loved Grandma Esther's visits. She looked forward to taking walks together, playing dress up, and helping Grandma make fancy outfits for her dolls. Most of all, she loved their quiet times when Grandma Esther would tell her stories about the "good old days"—when cars had running boards, milk came in glass bottles, and kids played hopscotch and jump rope. But her favorite stories were about

Prayed for Purse

answered prayers. Grandma Esther loved to pray. She talked to God about everything.

How Karlie wished she didn't have to share Grandma Esther with her cousins who lived in different parts of the country. Throughout the year, Grandma Esther spent time visiting each one. This summer was Karlie's turn.

That evening when Grandma Esther appeared in the airport corridor, Karlie wanted to run to her, but she couldn't go beyond the security guards. The moment her grandmother cleared the gates, Karlie threw herself into her grandmother's arms. Grandma gave her a great big hug. "Oh Karlie, I've missed you so much."

"I've missed you too, Grandma." Karlie reached for her grandmother's big black purse. Grandma never went anywhere without her homemade, quilted, black calico purse with leather drawstrings. Someday Karlie hoped to have one just like it. "Here, Grandma, let me carry your purse for you."

"It's pretty heavy, dear. Do you think you can manage?" Grandma asked.

"I can carry it for you," Dad volunteered after he greeted his mother with a hug and a kiss.

"No, I want to hold it," Karlie assured him. She heaved the drawstrings over her shoulder and grinned. "See? I told you I could carry it. It's not too heavy."

"Well, don't lose it, honey," Dad warned.

"I won't. I promise." Karlie gave her grandmother a reassuring smile.

By the time they found their car in the parking lot, Karlie was glad to hand the purse back. It had grown mighty heavy. Karlie snuggled close to her grandmother during the ride home, listening as the adults shared the

Prayed for Purse

latest news about the other members of the family. That night as Karlie climbed into bed, she said, "You know what, Grandma? When I grow up, I'm going to carry a big black purse just like yours."

Grandma chuckled, "Why wait until you're grown up? Tomorrow I'll make you one—your size, of course. How about that?"

"Really? That would be so cool!" Delighted, Karlie sighed and snuggled down to sleep.

Immediately after breakfast the next morning, Grandma kept her promise. First, she sorted through the fabric scraps she'd brought with her to make clothes for Karlie's dolls until she found a large swatch of quilted black calico. And then she cut the fabric into two squares and sewed them together. Grandma found another scrap of fabric—black nylon—and made a lining for the purse.

"What about the drawstrings?" Karlie asked, as the purse began to take shape.

"No problem." Grandma held up a leather cord. "I just happen to have a piece left over from when I made mine."

The purse was perfect, just the right size for Karlie to carry. She loved her new purse. What fun she had putting all her special things inside. Even her wallet fit perfectly. "You know, Grandma," Karlie commented, "I'm going to have this purse forever!"

One morning toward the end of the summer, Grandma announced at breakfast that she'd run out of embroidery thread. "Karlie, how would you like to walk to the store with me? Maybe we could do a little shopping."

"Oh, Grandma, I'd love that."

Karlie cleared the breakfast table in record time and then ran up the

Prayed for Purse

stairs to brush her teeth. She and her black calico purse were waiting at the front door when Grandma slipped on her favorite sweater and announced that she was ready to go.

Karlie skipped by Grandma's side, their purses swinging from their wrists. Inside the store, Grandma gave Karlie some money to buy whatever she wanted. Karlie's eyes danced with joy. She put the money in her wallet and slipped it back inside her purse.

Slowly she walked down the toy aisle, past the cars, trucks, and airplanes until she found doll accessories. First she chose a skirt and blouse for her doll but changed her mind. Grandma's doll clothes were nicer than the store-bought ones. She walked to the hair accessories aisle. Plastic combs, satin ribbons, barrettes, tiebacks for her ponytail—so many choices. In an aisle filled with books, she finally found what she wanted,

a storybook about wild horses. Karlie loved books; so did Grandma. She leafed through the pages and glanced at the pictures. It looked like an exciting story. Yes, she decided, this was exactly what she would buy with her money.

Karlie laid her purse down on the counter and handed the clerk the exact change. "I hope you enjoy your book," the clerk said, as she placed the book in a paper bag and handed it to Karlie. She eagerly reached for the bag and left the store with Grandma. On the way home, they stopped at the park to swing in the swings, watch the ducks swim in the pond, and even bought a popsicle at the ice cream stand.

When they got home, Karlie ran to show the book to her mother. Mom looked at it, and then glanced at the empty paper bag. "Karlie, where's your purse? Did you set it down somewhere when you came into the house?"

Prayed for Purse

"Oh, no!" Frantic, Karlie checked the paper bag and then ran to the front door where Grandma had left her own purse. Karlie's purse was not there. "I don't know where it is," she cried. "Grandma, did you see where I left my purse?"

"No, honey, I didn't. But don't worry. I'll help you look for it." Grandma Esther put her arm around Karlie's drooping shoulders. "You probably dropped it somewhere. We'll retrace our steps. I'm sure we'll find it."

On the way back to the store, Grandma and Karlie searched for the purse. Nothing. Inside the store, Karlie went up and down every aisle, past the toys, the doll section, the ribbons and barrettes, and to the shelves filled with books. No purse! Grandma asked the manager if anyone had turned in a child-sized purse like the one she was carrying.

"No, ma'am. I'm afraid not," he said. "But leave your phone number and if someone turns it in, I'll give you a call." Next they retraced their way through the park. No purse.

Karlie burst into tears. No one would return such a beautiful purse. She just knew it was gone forever. When she got home, Karlie ran into the living room and threw herself facedown on the sofa and cried.

Grandma sat down on a leather footstool next to the sofa and rubbed Karlie's back. "Honey, do you think Jesus knows where your purse is? Maybe we should ask Him to help you find it." Grandma knelt down beside the footstool. "Come, pray with me."

Karlie sniffed back her tears and knelt beside her grandmother. First Grandma prayed and then Karlie prayed, "Dear Jesus, please help me find my purse. Forgive me for being so careless. You know how much I love that purse. If someone finds it, please help them to be honest and bring

Prayed for Purse

it back to me." The words had barely escaped Karlie's mouth when the doorbell rang.

Grandma hurried to open the door. There stood a tall man wearing a jogging suit and a baseball cap. In his hand was Karlie's black calico purse. "I found this purse in the park and this address was in the wallet."

Karlie's eyes widened in surprise. "Oh, thank you! Thank you so much! God used you to answer my prayer."

After the kind man left, Grandma and Karlie knelt down and thanked God for helping an honest man find the purse and bring it back. That answered prayer made Karlie's faith grow stronger. She learned to not only be more careful with her possessions, but that she could talk to Jesus about anything—even a black calico purse. ■

And whatever you ask in My name, that I will do.
—John 14:13, NKJV

Zack's Secret

Zack looked around his room. It was a mess. He knew Mom had told him to get his room clean because Grandma was coming. He knew he should be making his bed, getting rid of the dust bunnies underneath it, and picking up his dirty clothes from his closet floor, but it was such a beautiful day. The last thing he felt like doing was cleaning his room.

What he really wanted to do was go outside and play with the new magnifying glass that he had gotten for his birthday. *Why does my room have to be cleaned now?* he thought. *It can wait. Grandma isn't coming until tomorrow. Besides, Mom is baking bread in the kitchen. She will never know if I go outside and have a little fun first. Then I'll sneak back into the house, pick things up, make my bed, and Mom will never know.*

Zack grabbed his magnifying glass, tiptoed down the hall, then looked both ways to make sure Mom was busy.

Zack's Secret

When he was sure she wouldn't notice him, he slipped out the door and closed it ever so quietly. At last, he was outside with his magnifying glass and a whole world of exciting things to explore.

After examining an ant, Zack studied a leaf. He then marveled at the beautiful design of the skin on his knee. He watched a worm dig in the soil and tried to catch a butterfly in the act of sucking nectar from a flower. Watching the worm had been easy. But the butterfly kept flying away.

That's when Zack remembered something a friend had told him about a magnifying glass. He had said that if a person took a magnifying glass and caught the sun's rays and focused them on a tiny spot, it would make that spot so hot that it would burn a hole in something or start a fire.

Zack wondered if it was really true. He just had to check it out! He knew he shouldn't play with matches or fire. That was dangerous. But he didn't have any matches and he wouldn't be playing with fire. He was just experimenting with his magnifying glass.

Can a magnifying glass really start a fire? he wondered. He was all alone on a patch of dry grass between the apartment where he lived and the small country hospital where his dad worked. It was a perfect place to try an experiment to see if what he had heard was really true. No one would ever know.

Zack bent low over the dry blades of grass as the very bright point of light under the magnifying glass began to darken the side of a small sliver of wood. A tiny bit of smoke popped into view, followed by another puff. Then another. It was working. It was working!

Then, *puff*! The smoke turned into a tiny column of fire so hot it made Zack jump back in surprise. In seconds, the column grew in size and

Zack's Secret

height, creating a very dark smoke that drifted with the gentle breezes blowing through the grass. He reached out to extinguish the fire, but it was already igniting nearby bushes and creating a lot of heat.

Zack stood up, his mouth hanging open. Maybe this hadn't been such a good idea. He started to scream for someone to help him put out the fire, then stopped. If he got caught, he was sure to get into trouble. No one had seen him, so he jumped up and ran as fast as he could toward home.

Mother saw Zack burst into the apartment and hurry toward his bedroom. She was about to remind him that his room still needed cleaning when she heard shouts from outside. Walking to the window, she saw people running toward the little plot of land by the road between the apartment building and the hospital. The grass was on fire! Flames lifted high into the afternoon air, and smoke was curling through the nearby trees. Some of the people were carrying buckets of water; others were beating the hot ground with wet blankets. Then, in the distance, she heard the wail of an approaching fire truck. Mother was very glad that Zack was safe and sound in his room.

That evening, after supper, Zack was sitting alone on his carefully made bed, feeling very, very uneasy. The fire had caused quite a stir in the neighborhood. Even students from the nearby high school had come to help fight the blaze. Now, all that remained of his "experiment" was a large blackened area where there used to be grass, bushes, and flowers. Everyone was asking, "How did it happen? What started the fire?"

It could have been a lot worse. Just across the street was the little hospital filled with sick people who couldn't run from the flames if the fire had spread. Zack's friend lived just down the road, and even his

Zack's Secret

apartment building would have proven to be no match for a fast-moving brushfire. People could have gotten hurt, or even worse, all because Zack did something really, really foolish. He should have known better. He should have realized the danger. He should have been cleaning his room as his mother had asked him to do.

"Zack?"

He looked up to find his father standing in the doorway.

"Zack, are you OK? You were so quiet during supper. Are you sick?"

Zack shook his head. "Dad, can I ask you something?"

"Sure."

Zack thought for a moment. "Remember how you said that Jesus is coming soon with His angels in the clouds of heaven and we need to be ready to meet Him?"

"Yes."

"What if—what if you did something kinda bad and then Jesus comes and He knows about it?"

Zack's father sat down beside his son. "Well, Jesus loves you so much that if you've done something wrong, He says He will forgive you if you just ask."

Zack sat staring into space.

"Let me ask you a question, Zack. You know that Grandma is coming tomorrow, right?"

"Yes."

"And, what if right before she came, you broke something that belonged to her. Do you think she would refuse to see you because of what you did?"

Zack shook his head. "No."

"Do you think she would still throw her arms around you and kiss you?"

Zack's Secret

"Of course," said Zack. "Especially if I said I was sorry."

"Well," said Dad. "Jesus is kinda like a grandma. He doesn't just love you when you're good and stop loving you if you've done something wrong. He loves you no matter what. And He is always willing to forgive you when you ask. What's really important to Jesus is that you love Him and want to live with Him forever—and that you learn from your mistakes."

A tiny tear dropped from Zack's eye as he sat in silence beside his dad. He wanted to be ready for Jesus to come. He wanted to live with Him forever. And he had certainly learned a big lesson about responsibility.

Zack stood to his feet and walked slowly across the room. Reaching into the top drawer of his dresser, he retrieved his shiny magnifying glass. "I've got to tell you something, Dad," he said quietly. "I just want you to know that I'm very, very sorry. I was playing with my magnifying glass to see if the sun could start a fire—and it did! Then I was scared I'd get caught, so I ran. I'm so sorry."

Dad put his arm around Zack. "Thanks for telling me. It makes you feel better when you get a secret like that off your chest, doesn't it? Fire is a dangerous thing, son, and should never be played with. We need to really thank Jesus that no one was seriously hurt."

"Yeah," said Zack. "I'm so glad Jesus protected everyone and that He still loves me even when I do things I shouldn't do."

"Me too," said Dad. "And I think you learned a valuable lesson."

Outside, as the sun was sinking behind the hills to the west, a tiny cloud drifted in the evening air. It wasn't Jesus and His angels, but if it had been, they would have found a boy who wasn't perfect, but who was working on it—and one that Jesus loved very, very much! ◼

> *We love Him because He first loved us.*
> —1 John 4:19, NKJV

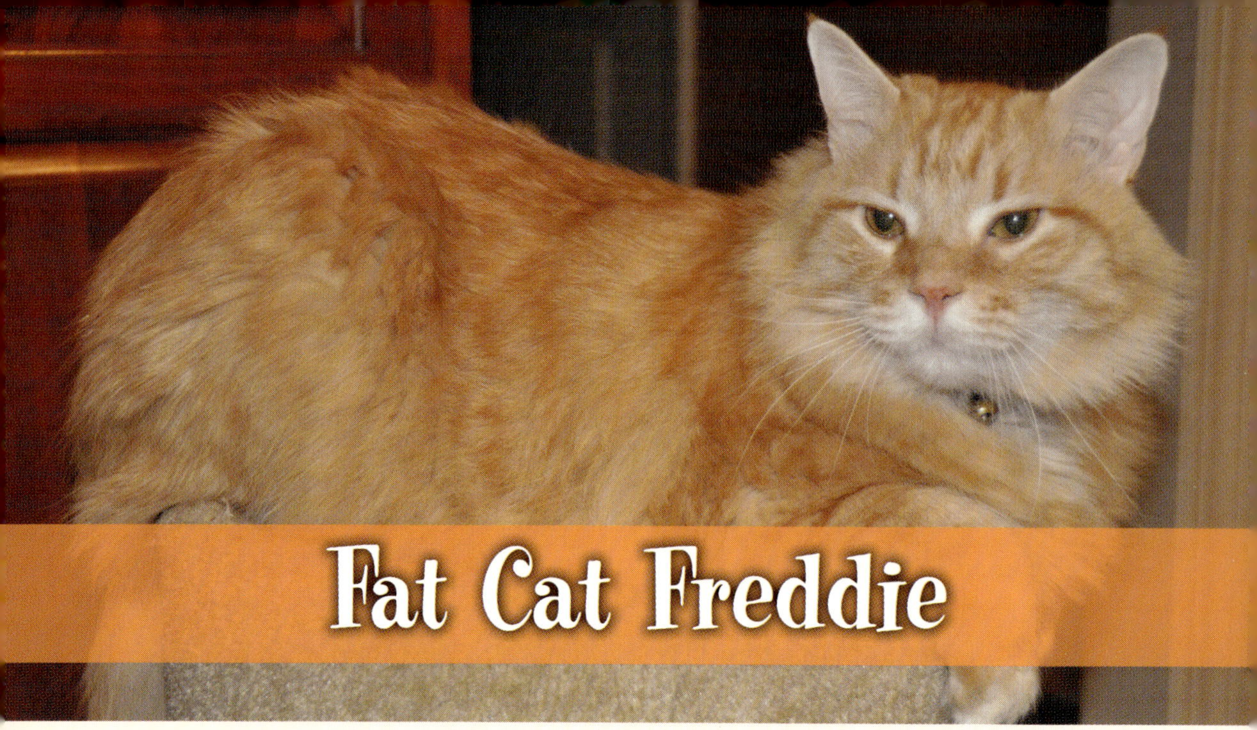

Fat Cat Freddie

Roy and Lisa thought Freddie was the best cat in the whole world! After all, he was a *prayed for* cat. They had prayed and prayed that someday they would have a cat of their own and they just knew God gave them Freddie!

They loved to play all the regular cat games with him. He chased a piece of thin rope they pulled through the house, and jumped and batted at a little cloth ball filled with catnip that they dangled from a string. They even dressed Freddie up in baby clothes—which was a fun game for the kids—but not so much fun for Freddie. The funniest thing of all, however, was watching Freddie chase the wind-up mouse and pounce on it.

In spite of all the exercise Freddie got at chasing things, he grew to be a fat cat—a very fat cat! He loved to sit in the big window where the sun would come streaming through. He would sleep there, stretch, give himself a bath, or just sit and look outside. Although

Fat Cat Freddie

he was an inside cat, the family had to really watch Freddie because he loved to escape to the outside whenever the door was opened.

One winter it snowed and snowed and snowed. There was so much snow that when the wind blew, it made giant snowdrifts that nearly covered the swing set. In fact, it snowed so much that the schools closed for a whole week, leaving the kids with plenty of time to play inside with Freddie and to play outside in the snow.

On one of the snow days, Lisa and Roy couldn't stand being inside another minute, so they put on their heavy snowsuits and went outside to build a snow fort. In some places, the snow was taller than them. All they had to do to make walls was shovel out the snow that was on the inside of the fort. They were just in the process of making a pile of snowballs in case they had to defend their fort, when Mom decided to brave the cold and get the mail.

Freddie watched Mom intently from his perch on the windowsill as she was getting on her heavy jacket, snow boots, and gloves. When she opened the front door, she was momentarily blinded by the intense glare of the sun shining on the bright snow. Freddie took advantage of the situation and ran out the door without anyone seeing him.

As Mom stomped through the deep snow to the end of the driveway, she had no idea Freddie was following her. She opened the mailbox, and just at that very moment, the big county snowplow went down their street. Snow went flying high up into the air.

The big truck made a terrible sound as it scraped the snow from the pavement. Freddie was so frightened he jumped into the wooden box for packages that was under the mailbox. At the same time, lots of the snow that flew up in the air came down and covered the box with a great

Fat Cat Freddie

big *swoosh*. There was so much snow that it almost covered the entire mailbox! After looking around and enjoying the glistening beauty of the sunshine, Mom went back inside. She had no idea that poor Freddie was trapped by the snow covering the wooden box.

Lisa and Roy had so much fun playing outside that it wasn't until after supper that Lisa went looking for Freddie. She looked in all the usual places: on top of the dresser, inside the clothes basket, under the bed, and behind the sofa. Where was Freddie?

Soon Roy joined the search. Roy even went to the door to call Freddie, in case he had escaped, as he sometimes did. But Freddie wasn't on the doorstep waiting to come in—as he usually was.

"Mom, have you seen Freddie?" Lisa asked.

"Not since early this morning, before you went out to build a fort. The last time I remember seeing Freddie, he was sitting on the windowsill."

They asked Dad, but he hadn't seen Freddie either.

Lisa started crying because she couldn't find Freddie and nobody remembered seeing him since early morning. How could he just disappear? Something terrible must have happened to him. He must have escaped when the door was open.

When it was time to go to bed, Mom, Dad, Lisa, and Roy had worship. They all prayed that Freddie would be safe and come home to them really soon. It was at bedtime that Freddie was missed the most because he usually slept at the foot of either Lisa's or Roy's bed. Now, there was no Freddie to keep them company.

After a couple of days, Lisa and Roy had to start school again; but every morning and every evening they prayed that Freddie would find his way home.

Fat Cat Freddie

One week went by and then another. Pretty soon sixteen days went by. The sun had been shining that day and the snow had started melting, but Freddie still had not come home. Lisa and Roy were very sad because they missed Freddie so much. They had almost given up hope of ever seeing their beloved cat again.

On the seventeenth day after Freddie had disappeared, Mom went out to the mailbox to get the mail. As she closed the lid, the snow that had built up around the mailbox fell away from the box under it—and out stepped Freddie! He had been in that box under the mailbox all that time! Mom was so happy to see Freddie! She picked him up, hugged and kissed him, and carried him all the way to the house. She could hardly wait to see the faces of Dad, Lisa, and Roy when they got home and saw Freddie.

Mom put some food down for him, and he was so hungry he immediately started to eat. It had been seventeen whole days since he had eaten anything! Mom was so excited she wanted to call the kids at school, but she decided to wait and tell them when they came home.

Around four o'clock that afternoon, Lisa and Roy came through the door, telling Mom all about what happened in school. They put their stuff away and went into the kitchen to talk to Mom some more. As they passed through the living room, they both saw Freddie at the same time. They stopped short and gasped, then started laughing and shouting, "Freddie, Freddie, you're home!" as they rushed over to hug him. Freddie was just as happy to see Lisa and Roy. He reached up and licked each of their noses, rubbed his head against them, and purred.

When Dad came home that night, Lisa and Roy met him at the door holding Freddie. Dad was amazed. Immediately, the family began to piece

Fat Cat Freddie

together the story of what had happened to their missing cat seventeen days before. Then, during family worship that night, they all thanked God for keeping Freddie safe and bringing him home.

It wasn't long before Freddie was sitting back in his favorite spot on the windowsill and enjoying the sun. But two things had changed: he wasn't quite as eager to escape as he once was, and he was no longer a fat cat! ∎

> *Call to Me, and I will answer you,
> and show you great and mighty things,
> which you do not know.*
> —Jeremiah 33:3, NKJV

Brave Kwame

Kwame was a new student in Mrs. Carlton's second-grade classroom. He and his family were refugees from Ghana in West Africa. They had just arrived in Australia and were sent to live in Tasmania—a little island below the Australian mainland. Nearly everything in Tasmania was new to Kwame: the school, the kids, the food, the games, and the language. Everything! And new things can sometimes be scary.

Kwame wouldn't play with the other kids at recess. He was shy. He couldn't speak the language they were using, and the games were all different from what he played in his homeland. The teacher encouraged the students to ask Kwame to play, but when they did, he always shook his head. He felt uncomfortable playing with them.

Because reading English was so difficult for Kwame, he participated very little during class. The teacher tried to help Kwame as much as she could, but she had twenty-four other

Brave Kwame

students as well. Kwame would open his books and try to read for most of the morning. But by lunchtime, he was tired of English and would sit in the reading corner, looking at picture books or just staring out the window for the rest of the day.

After a few weeks, the teacher became concerned about Kwame. Would he ever start talking? Would he learn English? How long would it be before he would read his books and do his work in class? She knew he could understand most of what she said to him. He had responded with a few words from time to time. But Mrs. Carlton knew that the only way Kwame was going to become comfortable speaking, reading, and writing English was if he tried. And right now, Kwame was too scared to even try.

One day, Mrs. Carlton talked to Kwame's mother after school. "Kwame needs to try," she said. "He is a good boy, but he is afraid to speak English or play with the other children. What can I do to help him?"

Kwame's mother listened carefully and then said, "Kwame is very talkative and lively at home where he feels comfortable. He just needs to be brave in new situations." Kwame was listening to the conversation. His mother bent down and talked softly to him about how important it was to be brave and at least try to speak English and play with the other children. Softly he replied, "I try."

But as the days went by, Mrs. Carlton could see that nothing was changing. Kwame needed help. She began to pray that something would happen that would give Kwame the confidence he needed to participate in school.

Then one warm afternoon, God answered her prayer with something completely unexpected. The students were sitting at their desks, doing

Brave Kwame

their worksheets. Kwame was looking at pictures in the reading corner. Suddenly, a little brown sparrow flew into the room through an open window. As the bird flew around the room, looking for somewhere to land, it flew so close to the students that they screamed and some even hid under their desks.

The little bird finally landed on a high bookshelf where it panted in distress. "Children, be quiet," Mrs. Carlton instructed. "The bird is frightened by your screaming."

Then, just as the children were calming down, a sparrow hawk—much bigger than the little sparrow—flew in through the same open window!

This time it wasn't just the kids who screamed. Mrs. Carlton let out a yelp and dove under her desk. The hawk landed on a low bookcase between the reading area and the children. It scanned the room full of frightened kids, one scared teacher, and one terrified sparrow. Clearly, the sparrow hawk had been chasing the sparrow and the little bird panicked and flew through the open window by accident. The hawk had followed without considering what might be on the other side of the window.

No one noticed Kwame in the reading corner. He hadn't screamed when the birds flew in. He hadn't hidden under a desk. Instead, he had watched calmly. And now, as the sparrow hawk stared at the sparrow across the room, Kwame quietly stood up. He was directly behind the hawk.

The other kids stuck their heads out from their hiding places to see the hawk and were surprised to see Kwame sneaking up behind it. The teacher peered out from underneath her desk. The entire class watched as Kwame inched closer and closer to the hawk.

Brave Kwame

"Mrs. Carlton," one of the students whispered, "make Kwame stop! He'll get bitten!"

Kwame took another step toward the sparrow hawk. His hands were coming up behind the bird.

Mrs. Carlton responded, "*Shhhhh,* I think Kwame knows what he's doing!"

And she was right! Kwame took one more step toward the sparrow hawk and, with a lightning-quick move, wrapped his hands around the wings of the hawk. The bird tried to bite his hands, but Kwame had grabbed it in just the right place so the hawk was unable to get to his fingers.

Kwame slowly walked to the window, held the hawk outside, and let it go. His hands were back inside in another lightning-quick move and the sparrow hawk flew away.

In the next few minutes, the students and teacher watched with astonishment as Kwame coaxed the little sparrow down from the shelf and caught it too. Five minutes after the two birds had flown into the classroom, they were both safely outside again.

Kwame had saved the day!

When Kwame turned back from the window, he was the center of attention. Amazed, the students began asking him questions. "How did you do that?" "Have you done that before?" "Where did you learn to catch birds?" "Was it scary?" "What did the hawk feel like?" "Did it bite you?"

Kwame listened to each of the questions and answered them in halting broken English. The students gave him time to form his answers. The words came slowly, and then faster and faster as Kwame became more

Brave Kwame

confident. Mrs. Carlton watched in amazement as Kwame went from being a shy, quiet boy to the talkative, lively boy his mother said he was at home.

Something had just happened that the teacher could have never planned. Kwame had become brave.

The fact is, Kwame had been brave all along. He just needed a couple of birds to help him show everyone else. And once his classmates knew just how brave he was, no one ever let him be shy again. After school, Kwame's bravery was the talk of all his classmates as they told their friends, their brothers and sisters, and their parents the amazing story of Kwame and the birds. The next day at school, Kwame was a hero. Everyone wanted to talk to him. And they all listened as he answered their questions.

Later that week, when Kwame was shopping with his family, he saw one of his classmates. The other boy tugged on his mom's coat, "Mom, that's him! That's Kwame—the boy who catches hawks! He's the bravest boy in our whole school!" ■

Watch, stand fast in the faith, be brave, be strong.
—1 Corinthians 16:13, NKJV

Tackle-Tag Disaster

"I'm so bored!" Hayley whined. "There's nothing to do." Hayley and her three brothers flopped down on the living room's shiny hardwood floor.

Jesse eyed the four pairs of new sneakers that were lined up by the front door. The shoes were special, not only because they were a gift from Papa, but because they had wheels that popped out on the bottom and they instantly became skates. "What would really be fun would be to use our new Heelys on this floor." He ran his hand over its slick surface. "I bet we could really fly."

"Bet so too," exclaimed Justin as he started lacing up his Heelys. And before long, all four children were zipping across the living room floor.

"Hey, this is fun!" the littlest brother, Noah, shrieked as he whipped around the corner of the sofa. Amid screeches and laughter, the skaters made a circular route around the sofa in the living room, down the hall,

Tackle-Tag Disaster

through the dining room, and back again. They were having so much fun they almost forgot their mother was folding clothes in the laundry room. After several minutes, the four children collapsed on the living room floor.

"Well, that was fun." Hayley knelt to adjust the ties on her Heelys. "What now?"

"I know!" exclaimed Jesse. "What if we play tackle tag?"

"Yeah," said Justin. "That sounds like lots of fun."

Jesse, Justin, Hayley, and Noah

Tackle tag was a favorite sport for the children, but they had never thought of playing the game on their Heelys, or in the house, for that matter.

An uneasy feeling came over Hayley. Not wanting to be left out, she eyed her brothers thoughtfully. "Do you think Mom will care?"

Justin wagged his head, "Naw, she won't care."

"*Shush!*" Jesse glanced toward the laundry room at the back of the house. "She'll hear you."

Noah piped up, "But didn't Mom say no skating in the house?"

Jesse laughed. "Hey, we've already done that and she didn't say anything. Besides, we'll be playing tackle tag—just on our Heelys, that's all. That's different, and besides, these are technically sneakers, right?"

Noah shot a worried look toward Hayley. She dropped her head. He and Hayley were the two who never liked to get into trouble.

"Come on, you guys. It will be fun." Jesse leaped to his feet and zipped around the living room door into the hall. Not to be outdone, the other boys followed, leaving Hayley with nothing to do but chase them. The four skaters circled through the hall and the dining room and back into the living room, skating wildly while trying to avoid getting tackled. Screams of laughter filled the house.

MISS BRENDA'S BEDTIME STORIES — VOLUME 1

Tackle-Tag Disaster

"Good thing Mom likes to listen to her iPod while she's working. She can't even hear us!" Hayley exclaimed.

Pow! Bang! Justin wasn't quick enough for his big brother Jesse and was easily tackled to the floor.

"Hey, that's a win for me!" Jesse gloated triumphantly.

Noah noticed Justin's face had a *I'm-going-to-get-you-back* kind of look. Their tag game was getting rough, and he didn't want to get into trouble. "I'm going to ask Mom if it's OK to play tackle tag in the house with our Heelys on!"

"Oh, don't be a tattletale," Hayley teased.

But Noah was determined. He'd just skated into the hall toward the laundry room when it happened. Justin, intent on getting his first "win," saw a perfect opening. While Jesse's back was turned toward Noah and Hayley, Justin skated as fast as he could across the hardwood floor and slammed smack into Jesse! Only instead of Jesse falling to the floor, the force of Justin's hit sent Jesse speeding into his bedroom—and right through the bedroom window. *Crash! Boom! Bang!* Like an explosion, the window shattered and glass flew everywhere!

For an instant, the children stared in disbelief and then began yelling. From the laundry room, Mom heard the blood-curdling screams and came running. She screeched to a halt inside the bedroom doorway. Her eyes widened in horror at the broken window and her son lying outside on the ground covered with blood.

"Quick, Hayley, get me a towel!" Mom shouted, running to Jesse. Hayley dashed into the bathroom and returned with a bath towel, throwing it through the open window at her mother below. Blood was squirting everywhere! Mom wrapped the towel around Jesse's bleeding arm. "Justin, quick, get me the phone. I need to call your grandfather."

Justin grabbed the phone from the other side of the bed. "Here, Mom, Papa will know what to do."

She fumbled as she punched out her father's cell phone number. "Please, Lord, let him pick up," she prayed.

"Hello," Papa answered on the first ring.

Tackle-Tag Disaster

Breathless with fright, Mom told him everything. "Hurry, Dad. Jesse is bleeding badly!"

Fortunately, Papa was just returning from town, so he wasn't far away.

While they waited for Papa, the kids had time to think about what they had done. They knew the rule—no skating indoors—and they shouldn't have been roughhousing! Now Jesse was hurt and bleeding. *Maybe he was going to die!* "Oh, Mom, we are so sorry," they said again and again.

After what seemed like an eternity, Papa arrived and helped Jesse into his truck, along with Mom and the other children. By now, the towel Mom held on Jesse's arm was soaked with blood. And Jesse was bleeding from the cuts on his stomach as well.

Jesse, Melody, Noah, Hayley, Danny Shelton (Papa), and Justin

From the truck, Papa made a quick call to Dr. Samuel, the local doctor. "Meet me at the clinic!" Dr. Samuel ordered.

When Papa brought the truck to a stop in front of the clinic, Dr. Samuel hadn't yet arrived. Jesse's arm was still bleeding badly. Remembering that Miss Brenda was a registered nurse and lived near the clinic, Papa shifted the truck into gear and headed for her apartment. "Miss Brenda will know what to do!"

The truck had barely left the clinic's parking lot when Noah shouted, "Hey, Papa, there's Miss Brenda! She's driving toward us!"

Papa honked his horn while the kids wildly waved for her to stop. Miss Brenda pulled up beside them and rolled down her window. All the children began shouting at once. Papa motioned for them to be quiet. Taking a deep breath, he quickly relayed what had happened.

"Meet me inside the clinic!" Miss Brenda shouted as her car surged forward into the clinic's parking lot.

Tackle-Tag Disaster

Once inside, Miss Brenda and Papa rushed Jesse into an examination room while Mom stayed in the waiting room with the other children. Miss Brenda elevated Jesse's arm and applied pressure to the bloody towel.

A few minutes later, Dr. Samuel came rushing in. Miss Brenda could see the fear in Jesse's eyes when Dr. Samuel began to clean the wound, so she started telling him funny stories. In fact, she never quit talking as Dr. Samuel stuck Jesse with a needle to inject some numbing medicine and then stitched up his wound. By the time Dr. Samuel finished bandaging it, everyone was laughing, including Mom, who had to come in to see what was so funny.

Dr. Samuel looked seriously at Mom and the kids, "Jesse's a very lucky boy! He severed a large blood vessel and this could have been very serious."

Papa shook his head, "No, not lucky. I believe Jesse's guardian angel flew through that window with him and protected Jesse from getting hurt any worse."

That night when Mom talked with the kids about the day's events and their disobedience for skating inside the house, she reminded them of the story of Satan's disobedience. "Even though God loved Lucifer, He had to banish him from heaven forever. There are always consequences when we choose to disobey. And even though you're sorry, a consequence still hurts, doesn't it?" she asked Jesse.

Jesse nodded. His eyes grew wide and dark. "Mom, what's going to happen to us for disobeying you? Are we going to get punished?"

She smiled and placed a big kiss on Jesse's forehead. "I think you've all suffered enough consequences for your disobedience for one day." Then they knelt down and asked Jesus to forgive them, and Mom prayed, "Thank You, Jesus, for protecting Jesse."

"OK, kids, it's time for your showers,"

Tackle-Tag Disaster

Mom announced. Jesse's shower took much longer than usual. Mom had to carefully remove lots and lots of tiny pieces of glass from his hair and his clothing. And with each shard, Jesse relearned the lesson that it's better to obey than to have to suffer the consequences. ■

> *Children, obey your parents in the Lord, for this is right.*
> —Ephesians 6:1, NIV

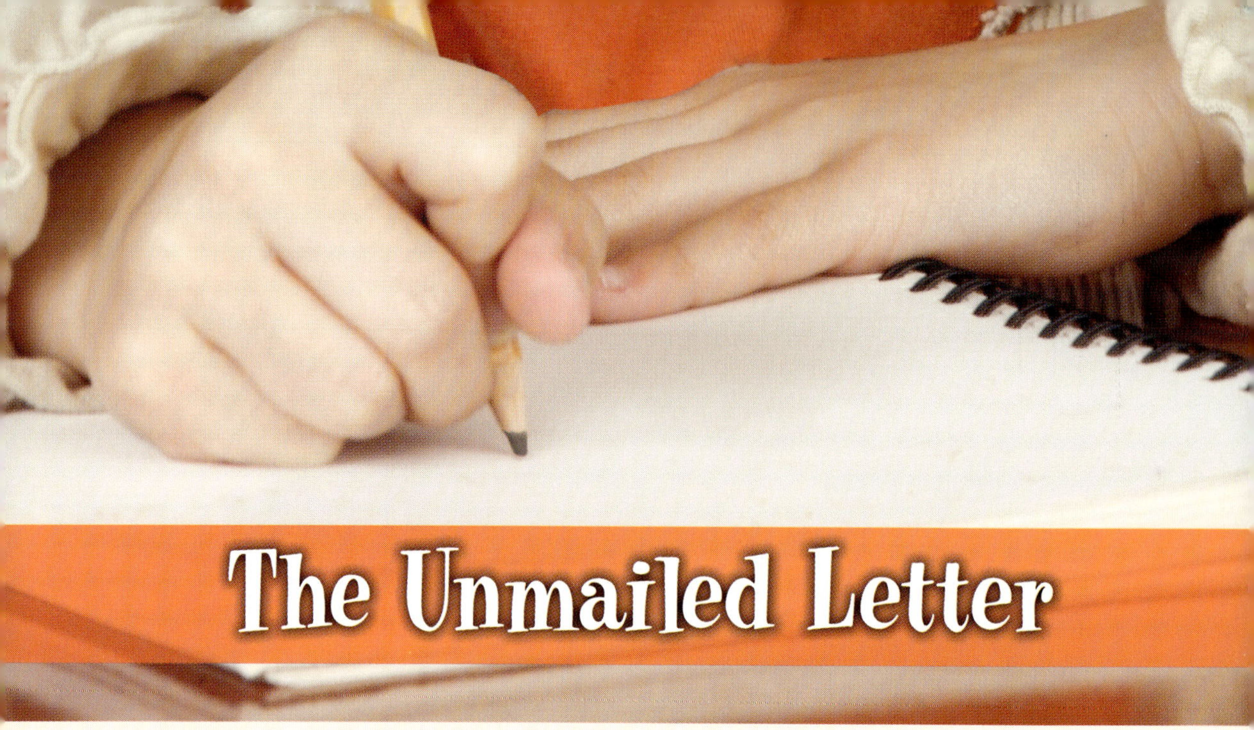

The Unmailed Letter

Holly's troubles started the day she and her best friend, Cheri, tried out for the lead in the school play. When Cheri got the part, Holly hid her disappointment. She tried to be happy for her friend. She really did!

As the only fourth-grader chosen to be in the school play, Cheri was nervous that she might make a mistake in front of the older kids. To make Cheri feel better, Holly volunteered to help her memorize her lines.

At first, all went well. With Holly's help, Cheri memorized her lines perfectly. But as the weeks passed, Cheri became friends with the other cast members—especially Lynn, a giggly girl in the fifth grade. They began hanging out during recess and after school. Whenever Holly suggested she and Cheri walk home or study together in the evening, Cheri always claimed to be too busy. The breaking point for

The Unmailed Letter

Holly was when she asked to sit at Cheri's table in the cafeteria.

"Oh," Cheri responded nervously, "I'm saving that place for Lynn."

Holly could think of nothing else all afternoon. In English class, she didn't care about verb tenses. She felt tense enough on her own. By the time Holly got home from school, her hurt had turned into fury. And as usual, she poured out her frustrations to her mother.

"Can you imagine? Cheri and I have been best friends since preschool and she treats me like this?" Holly was so angry that if she'd been a cartoon character, the artist would have drawn smoke coming out of her ears.

Holly's mother listened carefully, then made a strange suggestion. "I think you need to write Cheri a letter telling her what you just told me. Tell her exactly how you feel about the way she has been treating you."

Holly couldn't believe she'd heard her mother correctly. "You do? Can I say anything I want?"

"Absolutely!"

Holly's frown blossomed into a broad smile. "All right! I'm really going to tell her off. She'll be sorry she ever treated me like that!"

Holly didn't stop to wonder why her mother suggested such a thing. She charged up the stairs to her room. "I'll tell her just how I feel! You bet I will!"

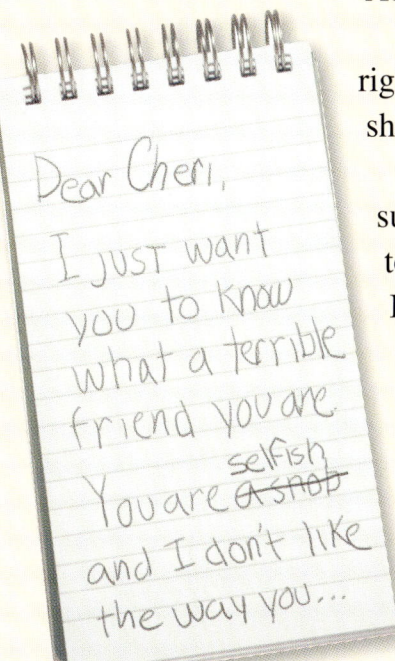

Grabbing a pad of paper and a pen from her desk drawer, she curled up on her bed. Her pen raced across the page as she poured out her anger one word at a time. Pleased with her masterpiece and feeling much better, Holly smiled to herself. *That will teach Cheri a lesson! She'll be sorry!*

Holly leaped from her bed and ran down the stairs two at a time. She found her mother vacuuming the floor in the family room. "Mom, wanna hear what I wrote?" Holly shouted.

The Unmailed Letter

Her mother turned off the vacuum. "Sure."

Holly's voice filled with passion and fury as she read the letter aloud to her mother. When she finished, she asked, "So, what do you think?"

"Great job, honey. You told her off all right, in no uncertain terms. Good writing too. I could truly feel your frustration. Now, I want you to take the letter into the kitchen, tear it up into little pieces, and throw it into the trash can."

"What?" Holly screeched. "But you said I did a great job. You told me to write the letter, remember?"

"Yes, I did," her mother admitted. "Did writing it make you feel better?"

"Well, yeah, I guess so." Holly could see where this was going.

"Then the letter served its purpose, so throw it away. The wisest man who ever lived said that only a fool speaks (or writes) in haste. And an angry man only stirs up conflict."

"But, she can't get away with treating me like that. I want to give her a piece of my mind."

"Honey, sending the letter to Cheri will not help the situation between you and your friend, will it? It could do the exact opposite. You'd probably lose a friend forever. Would you want that to happen?"

"No," Holly mumbled, "but I'd feel a whole lot better."

Mom smiled. "You already feel better just having written it, right?" She took a short breath before continuing. "Cheri is acting a little foolish right now. A good friend will realize that Cheri's success is affecting her better judgment and you need to be patient with her. My guess is that in time she'll be your friend again, especially after the play ends and the older kids go back to their everyday activities."

The Unmailed Letter

"But-But-But what can I do?" Holly felt hurt and confused.

"Nothing right now. Just be nice to her. Treat her with kindness. Send her a note saying that you know she'll do a great job in the play," Mom suggested. "Until Cheri discovers how inconsiderate she's being, hang out with your other friends like Karen or Maggie."

"But," Holly's lower lip began to quiver, "what if she never, ever …" Holly couldn't make herself say the awful words.

Mom gently caressed Holly's shoulder. "If that happens, you will have to admit to yourself that Cheri wasn't the great friend you thought she was, and find others to take her place. But knowing Cheri as I do, I don't think that will happen."

"I hope you're right, Mom. I can't imagine not being best friends with Cheri. I really can't."

"I know," Mom gazed into Holly's sad brown eyes. "Like it or not, you can never make someone love you. They have to want to. That's just life!"

Holly followed her mother's advice. She tearfully tore up the hateful note and tossed it into the garbage can. With a heavy heart, she watched as Cheri chummed around with her new fifth-grade friends. Whenever Cheri glanced her way, Holly managed to put a smile on her face as if nothing was wrong.

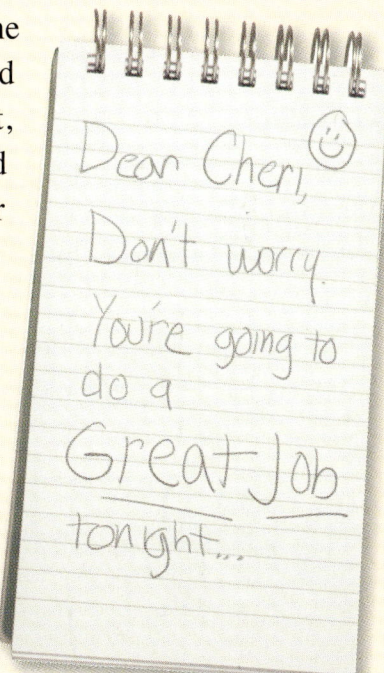

On the evening of the Christmas program, Holly wrote a second letter and slipped it into Cheri's hand just before the play began. "Dear Cheri," the note said, "Don't worry. You're going to do a great job tonight. You've practiced your lines and worked hard. I'm proud of you. Go out there and wow the audience for our class. Show them what a fourth-grader can do. Your best friend, Holly."

The Unmailed Letter

When Cheri walked out onto the stage, her gaze swept across the audience and stopped when she spotted Holly. Holly grinned and gave her friend a thumbs up. Even from where Holly sat in the third row, she could see Cheri's eyes fill with tears. Cheri paused a moment and then spoke her opening lines.

Throughout the play, Holly silently cheered her friend. *Wow! She's good. Now I can see why Mr. Hansen gave Cheri the part.*

The curtain fell to a thunderous applause, and no one applauded louder than Holly. By the time Holly pushed her way backstage, a crowd of fans surrounded Cheri. *I guess I'll have to wait until tomorrow to congratulate her.* Holly sighed and turned to leave. Suddenly, a hand grabbed her shoulder.

"Hey, wait!" Cheri pleaded, her face gleaming with the glow of success. "Where are you going so fast?"

Holly couldn't speak as Cheri threw herself into her friend's arms. The two girls hugged each other and twirled about, both talking at the same time.

"I've been a jerk to you these last few days and I'm so sorry," Cheri admitted as the crowd thinned out. "It would serve me right if you never wanted to be my friend again."

Holly's eyes filled with tears. "It's OK. I've done some dumb things in the past too. Hey, where are your new friends?"

"They're having a cast party at the ice cream shop tonight." Cheri curled her lip.

Holly frowned. She couldn't understand the sudden change in her friend. "Hey, I don't want to keep you. You go ahead. We can catch up tomorrow."

Cheri shook her head. "They don't want me along. They didn't say so, but I guess they were jealous when Mr. Hansen called me back on stage for a second bow. Talk about jerks! Wait until I tell you what Lynn said after the show!"

The Unmailed Letter

As they walked away arm in arm, Holly couldn't help but think, *How did Mom get to be so smart?*

As she listened and laughed at Cheri's wild backstage stories, Holly was so thankful that she didn't send her first letter. And then she made a mental note to herself, *Thank Mom for being so wise.* ◼

*Do you see a man who speaks in haste?
There is more hope for a fool than for him. . . .
An angry man stirs up dissension,
and a hot-tempered one commits many sins.*
—Proverbs 29:20, 22, NIV

Maxwell, the *Kids' Time* Dog

Miss Brenda stepped back to view the new set for *Kids' Time,* a children's program on 3ABN (Three Angels Broadcasting Network). *The set is much bigger than the old one,* she thought. *We'll be able to have lots of kids on the show.* Miss Brenda was the producer and host of the program.

Brad Walker, the *Kids' Time* director, walked up beside her. "Isn't it beautiful?" Miss Brenda exclaimed. "Did you ever dream we would have anything this wonderful?"

"Yes, it's beautiful," Brad responded, "but there is something missing."

"Like what?"

"I don't know, but the set doesn't look *kid friendly.* Maybe you should add some toys, like a bike, a swing in the yard, or a basketball hoop."

Miss Brenda thought for a moment and then shook her head. "No, I don't want toys on the set. When I first agreed to produce *Kids' Time,* God impressed

The new Kids' Time *set.*

Maxwell, the *Kids' Time* Dog

me that the set should be about two things: God's Bible and God's book of nature. We may have a new set, but God hasn't changed His instructions to me. We don't need toys to let kids know Jesus loves them." She shook her head a second time. "No, definitely not toys!"

"Well then, you should at least get a dog," he said emphatically.

"If I had to choose between toys and a dog, then it would have to be a dog!" Miss Brenda replied without thinking.

Miss Brenda with Kids' Time *director, Brad Walker*

"That's a great idea! Go find us a dog!" Brad smiled and walked away.

Oh no! thought Miss Brenda, *What did I just say? Not a dog! Please Lord, not a dog!* You see, Miss Brenda was afraid of dogs. Actually, she's afraid of lots of animals, but especially dogs! How was she ever going to survive with a real, live dog on the set?

Miss Brenda began to pray, "Please dear Jesus, You know how I feel about dogs, but if You want a dog on the program, please help us find the right one. We need a dog that is quiet because if it barks a lot, we wouldn't be able to tape the show. And if it's not too much trouble, can You please give us a dog that won't lick me or jump up on me? Oh, and one more thing, Jesus, can You help me to not be afraid? I love You so much and I want to do Your will, so please give me the courage I will need. Thank You, Jesus. Amen."

Miss Brenda could hardly sleep that night just thinking about what it would be like with a dog on the program, and how she would have to pray every minute of the day to be in the same room with the animal—much less to tape a show with the dog on the set.

The next day, Miss Brenda asked if anyone knew of a nice, quiet dog that would be good for *Kids' Time*. Several crew members brought their dogs for Miss Brenda to "interview." However, as soon as a dog got close

Maxwell, the *Kids' Time* Dog

to her, she would scream and run out of the room!

Orangevale Girls' Chorus with Brad Davis singing on Kids' Time

The cameramen laughed and shook their heads, telling each other, "I don't think this is going to work. A dog sitting next to Miss Brenda? Nope! It won't ever happen!"

Miss Brenda continued to pray that God would choose the perfect dog for *Kids' Time*. Dog after dog came and went. None of them seemed to be the right one!

On the first day of taping, there was still no dog. A beautiful doghouse was on the set, but it was empty.

After the second day of taping, Brad spoke to Miss Brenda. "I can't keep showing a doghouse without a dog, so the programs are not going to be very good if I have to keep staying on close-up shots. You really need to find a dog," he pleaded.

"I've been praying about it, but I just can't seem to find the right one," replied Miss Brenda.

"I agree with you, however, we need to find one as soon as possible."

She paused and bit her lip. "Miss Jeannie from the *Tiny Tots* program called me and said that on the news last night she saw a black Labrador Retriever that needs a home. I'm going to the animal shelter with our cameraman, Mitch Owen, to see the dog."

Cameraman Mitch Owen with Miss Brenda.

"That's great! I hope it works out." Brad chuckled to himself as he walked away, thinking, *She's never going to find a dog!*

Maxwell, the *Kids' Time* Dog

Miss Brenda hurried to the parking lot to catch up with Mitch. "Are you ready to go?"

"Sure am. Aren't you riding with me?" he asked.

"Well, that depends." Miss Brenda walked slowly toward her own car. "Is there a chance that we are coming back with a dog?"

"Well, yes, that's why we're going, aren't we?" Mitch looked confused.

"Of course! And that's why I'll follow you in my car. There's no way I'm going to ride in the same car with any dog!" Miss Brenda gave a nervous giggle.

Mitch shook his head and laughed. "OK. It's about a twenty minute ride to Du Quoin from here."

When they entered the animal shelter and met Amanda Creely, one of the shelter's directors, Miss Brenda was not prepared for what she saw: a long sidewalk lined with large see-through, metal dog cages, containing all kinds of dogs. And they were all barking!

Miss Brenda gasped and began to shake with fear. The louder the dogs barked, the more she shook. *Oh my! It sure stinks in here!* Miss Brenda tried to hold her breath or at least not breathe in too deeply. Amanda and Mitch followed right behind her.

As Miss Brenda passed one cage, a big yellow boxer let out a loud growl. Terrified, Miss Brenda threw her arms around Amanda and hung on for dear life! Startled, Amanda almost lost her balance and burst out laughing.

"Are you sure you want a dog?"

"*Nooooo,* I'm sure I d-don't want a dog," Miss Brenda stuttered. She released her hold on the shelter director and took a deep breath. "But I'm sure God wants one for *Kids' Time*."

Maxwell, the *Kids' Time* Dog

Dr. Calvin Taylor plays for Aileana, while the floor director, Larry McLucas, gives direction.

Still laughing, Amanda said, "Why don't you go wait in the lobby and I'll bring a dog to you."

"I-I-I think that's probably a good idea." Poor Miss Brenda was so scared that she couldn't stop trembling. When she sat down on a chair in the lobby, her legs shook so much that her high heels clicked on the tile floor.

A few minutes later, the door between the lobby and the kennels opened. Amanda and Mitch appeared with a large black Lab. The dog ambled over to Miss Brenda, who was too scared to even scream. He didn't bark. He didn't jump on her or try to lick her. He didn't pester her at all! The dog eyed Miss Brenda for a few seconds and then lay down by her feet and fell asleep. Miss Brenda sat still for a long time with the dog at her feet. Only when she stood up did the black Labrador wake up. When Miss Brenda walked across the room, the dog followed her. And when she stood talking with Amanda, he lay down by her feet and went to sleep again.

Overjoyed, Miss Brenda knew this was the dog for *Kids' Time*! Jesus had answered her prayer! All the way home, she prayed, "Thank You, dear Jesus, for giving us just the right dog!"

The next day, when the black Lab came to the set, everyone fell in love with him. The dog seemed to enjoy being on the program and didn't mind being positioned one way or another for the right camera shots. He never once barked, whined, or complained. He loved the children, but what he enjoyed most was sleeping. Before Larry McLucas, the floor director, could finish his count to start the program, "Five, four, three, two . . . ," the dog put his head down, closed his eyes, and went to sleep! Brad wanted to get a camera shot with the dog's head up and awake, but it was almost impossible.

Maxwell, the *Kids' Time* Dog

Tyler Walker helps keep Maxwell awake.

Tyler, the director's son, became the official "dog watcher." It was his job to wake up the dog when a close camera shot was needed. Sometimes he would have to hide in the doghouse to do this. If you were on the set, watching closely, you could see Tyler's hand come out of the doghouse to wake up the dog and then when Tyler heard the director tell him over his headset, "Hurry, get your hand back in the house, I'm taking the shot," Tyler would quickly pull his hand inside before the camera was able to see him.

The dog needed a name so Miss Brenda put a notice on the Internet for people to send in suggestions. Thousands of names poured in from around the world. At the end of the dog's first week at work, the name with the most votes was Maxwell—or Max, for short—after the famous children's author, Arthur Maxwell, whose stories have blessed so many children.

The next thing Max needed was a home. Miss Brenda traveled too much to take good care of a dog, so Jorge and Lynette Jaque and their two children, Noelia and Sebastian, invited Maxwell to live with them, where he could get lots of attention.

Jorge, Lynette, Noelia, and Sebastian with Maxwell

Now Maxwell is a "celebrity dog" for Jesus. He is loved by kids all over the world and gets fan mail every day. Best of all, Jesus answered Miss Brenda's prayers. She is not afraid of Maxwell—no, not one bit. In fact, she loves Max. They have become great friends. Miss Brenda pets him, gives him treats, and he wears a special *Kids' Time* scarf that matches the color of whatever Miss Brenda is wearing.

Maxwell, the *Kids' Time* Dog

Maxwell at work on the Kids' *Time* set.

Maxwell loves to "work" on the *Kids' Time* set, and he loves his new family. He also loves the children he meets. But most of all, Maxwell loves to sleep! ■

The LORD is my helper; I will not fear. What can man [or animals] do to me?
—Hebrews 13:6, NKJV

The Spelling Champion

Karen closed her eyes tight and pictured the word in her mind. Carefully, she spelled the word out, one letter at a time. When she opened her eyes, her teacher was smiling at her.

"Congratulations, Karen. That's correct. You are the sixth-grade spelling champion for our school."

Karen couldn't wait to get home and tell her mom and dad the exciting news. As spelling champion, she not only got a beautiful certificate, but, in just a few weeks, she would represent her school at the regional championships.

During the following weeks, Karen concentrated hard on her spelling. Her mom tested her every night and she even mastered tricky words such as *receive* and *icicle*. Finally, she was ready.

Karen and her mom arrived at the town hall for the regional spelling championship. There were excited children and parents everywhere. The

The Spelling Champion

building was old and beautiful, with high ceilings and stained-glass windows. The center of the great hall was covered by an enormous dome. The sun shone through the dome, and sunlight danced across the children and parents who were talking in noisy clusters. Karen tried not to think about how nervous she was. She held her mom's hand tight as she registered and put on her name tag.

Karen and her mom found a seat in the middle of the room and sat down, ready for the championship to begin. Karen tried to remember how to spell some of her favorite words, but the letters were a jumbled mess in her mind. She held on to her mother's hand even tighter and tried to ignore her heart pounding in her ears.

Finally, it was Karen's turn. Her mom squeezed her hand and whispered, "Good luck!" Karen found her place at the table with the seven other spelling champions from different schools and tried to listen to the instructions. Her heart was beating so loudly she wondered if she'd be able to hear.

"Children," said the teacher in charge, "I'm going to read each word once, then say the word in a sentence, then read it alone again. You need to write each word on a separate piece of paper in front of you. When you have finished, cover your work until I ask you to put your pens down. You will have thirty seconds to write each word. At the end, I will ask you to hold up your paper. This is an elimination tournament. Those people who have correctly spelled the word will progress to the next round. Those who spell the word incorrectly will be asked to return to their seats for the remainder of the program. Any questions?"

Karen breathed slowly. Her teacher had practiced this exact format with her so she knew what to expect. All she had to do was picture the words in her mind and she would be fine. She closed her eyes and said a prayer asking God to be with her. She wanted to do her very best.

The Spelling Champion

"Round one," said the teacher in charge. "*Surprise*. Your word is *surprise*." The teacher paused for a moment to let the children think. "*Surprise*. I went to a *surprise* birthday party." Karen didn't wait for her to say it again. She knew how to spell *surprise*. A little bubble of excitement welled up inside her. *This is going to be easy,* she thought. *I might win this contest after all.*

Using a sharpened pencil, Karen carefully wrote the letters S-U-R-P-R-I-S-E on her piece of paper. She put down her pencil, placed her hand over her piece of paper, and smiled. *This is a piece of cake! I thought it would be harder than this!* She imagined herself standing up in front of all the children and parents and being awarded the prize for regional spelling champion. The prize was fantastic. She would win a gold trophy with a dictionary mounted on the top, and her name would be engraved on the base. Her school library would win five hundred dollars in prize money, and Karen herself would win one hundred dollars in book coupons from her favorite bookstore.

Karen heard the teacher's voice one last time. "*Surprise*. Your word is *surprise*. You have thirty seconds."

That thirty seconds took a long time to pass. Karen checked her paper one more time, sure that she was right. Or was she? A tiny weed of doubt began to grow inside her. Karen started to wonder, *Did I spell it correctly?* It looked right, but maybe it was wrong. If only there was some way to check. If only there was some way to know for sure.

That's when it happened. Out of the corner of her eye, Karen saw that the boy sitting next to her had finished writing his word. But instead of covering his paper up like the teacher said, he leaned back in his chair and

The Spelling Champion

closed his eyes. Karen could see big black letters on the piece of paper in front of him. She argued with herself for a moment. *I know it isn't right to look at someone else's work, but maybe this is different. I already spelled the word on my paper. Maybe it isn't so bad if I just want to check to see if I have it right. It isn't really cheating, is it?*

So, with just a few seconds to go, Karen glanced over at the boy's paper next to her and saw that he had written something different: S-U-P-R-I-S-E. Karen started to panic. Whose was right? Was hers right or was his right? She wasn't sure anymore. *Did* surprise *have two R*s *or just one?*

"Ten seconds," said the teacher.

Karen had to make a quick decision. Overwhelmed with doubt, she grabbed her pencil and scribbled over the top of S-U-R-P-R-I-S-E.

Underneath, she quickly wrote S-U-P-R-I-S-E.

"And pencils down," said the teacher. "Now, please hold up your papers for us to see."

The paper felt heavy in Karen's hands. She held it up in front of her and waited for the teacher to continue.

"The correct spelling of *surprise* is S-U-R-P-R-I-S-E. I'm sorry, Karen and David, you have both been eliminated."

Tears prickled at the edges of Karen's eyes. She had been eliminated in the very first round. She looked at the hard, wooden floor as she scurried back to her place in the audience. When her mother gave her a comforting hug, Karen burst into tears.

She had spelled the word correctly the first time. If only she hadn't given in to the temptation to cheat, she would have still been in the competition. For the rest of the day, Karen had to sit and listen to round

The Spelling Champion

after round of contestants; and in each round she knew how to spell every single word. If she hadn't cheated, she might have made it to the finals. Instead, she was in the audience, embarrassed and upset at what she had done.

Karen learned a hard lesson that day and she never made the same mistake again. She also never forgot how to spell *surprise*.

> *Blessed is the man [kid]...*
> *in whose spirit there is no deceit.*
> —Psalm 32:2, NKJV

The Unwanted Train

It was, without a doubt, the most incredible, most awesome, most totally cool train set Jacob had ever seen. The big black engine puffed smoke and whistled loud and long as it pulled swaying coal cars and low-riding flat cars around the shiny silver track. Boxcars lined the sidings, and at each crossing, lights flashed and little wooden arms dropped to warn miniature automobiles and their tiny drivers to stop. Towns and farms trembled at the passing of the heavy engine and its line of clickety-clackety cars. Painted cows watched silently as the mighty caravan swept past. The Santa Fe Express was coming through!

A tall, well-dressed man stopped and stood beside Jacob, admiring the curving tracks and colorful collection of houses and barns. Then he walked over to the salesperson waiting nearby and, in a matter-of-fact voice, said, "I'll take it."

Of course you'll take it, Jacob thought to himself. *Who wouldn't? It's*

74   MISS BRENDA'S BEDTIME STORIES — VOLUME 1

The Unwanted Train

the most wonderful, most exciting, most terrific train set in the whole world. Anyone with half a brain would jump clean out of his skin to get it for Christmas. Then he sighed, his ten-year-old stomach simply aching with desire.

Just then, his dad entered the toy store, arms filled with odd-shaped packages. "Dad," Jacob called, running to meet him, "I know what I want for Christmas." He motioned toward the table by the window. "Just look at that!"

Dad stared in the direction his son was pointing, then glanced down at Jacob. "You want a baby doll that wets its pants and cries 'Mama'?"

"No," Jacob grimaced. "To the right. Over to the right."

"You want a pink umbrella with kittens on it?"

"Dad!" Jacob groaned between clenched teeth. "On the table. Look on the table!"

"Oh," Dad said, walking toward the train display. "Hey, this is nice. It's got everything—little roads, stop signs, cows. It's a Lionel too. They're the best, you know. Been around for years."

Jacob nodded enthusiastically. "And Dad," he urged, "see that man over there? He just walked up to the salesperson and said, 'I'll take it.' You could do that too. Just say, 'I'll take it.' It's that simple!"

Jacob walked away from the display, leaving his dad bending low, studying the price tag hanging on the little red station by the freight yard. Jacob smiled to himself. *Yup. Christmas is going to be extra special this year.*

Christmas Eve finally arrived. Jacob was more than happy to sing carols, pop popcorn, eat his favorite holiday desserts, and play board games with his family—anything to help keep his mind off the much anticipated event that would take place with the rising sun. All he could

The Unwanted Train

think of was the train—the awesome train that he'd find waiting for him when he came down the stairs in the morning.

When bedtime finally arrived, Jacob dragged himself up to his room and soon fell into a restless sleep. Steam engines chased each other around and around in his dreams.

"Wake up, Jacob. It's Christmas!" His younger sister's cheery voice rang out from the doorway. Jacob's eyes fluttered open. Yes. *Yes!* At long last, it was time to graciously accept his wonderful, exciting, incredible, fantastic, awesome Lionel train set! Pausing at the top of the stairs in his pajamas, he did his best to prepare himself for what lay ahead. He must present a proper mixture of surprise and pleasure without actually fainting. He knew that parents liked to see their children's faces overflow with joy on Christmas morning.

Taking a curious, yet innocent pose, he crept down the stairs. Dad was waiting at the bottom with a broad smile wrinkling his cheeks. "Merry Christmas, Jacob," he said. "We have a big surprise for you." Dad motioned toward the tree. There, rumbling around on shiny, silver tracks was a steam engine pulling a line of boxcars.

Jacob rushed across the room and dropped to his knees beside the rolling train. "Oh, Dad," he gushed, "it's beautiful! It's just what I—"

Wait a minute. There's something wrong here. The engine wasn't as magnificent as Jacob remembered. The wheels weren't as detailed; the cars not as colorful and real looking. Even the little station had painted windows, not cutout ones like he'd seen in the toy store. This wasn't his train. This wasn't a Lionel!

"Do you like it?" Dad asked. "I wanted to buy the one you showed me, but it cost much more than we could afford. With your brothers in college

The Unwanted Train

and you and your sister growing out of your clothes every six months, we simply don't have any extra money."

Jacob sat in silence.

"Besides," Dad continued, "I think it's a nice set. Look, it came with a couple logs for the flatcar." He paused, "I know it's not a Lionel, son, but it's a nice train, right?"

Jacob's Christmas dreams had been shattered. This was not the train he wanted. But a little voice seemed to be speaking to him from somewhere deep in his disappointment. It was saying that the right thing to do was to graciously accept what was real, even when dreams are more fun and more exciting. Things can't always be the way we want them to be; a father's loving sacrifice is more valuable than a son's selfish desire.

He watched the little train puff its way around the base of the Christmas tree. The whistle blew long and loud. "Dad," Jacob said, looking up into the face of the man who had given him the best that he could, "it's the most wonderful train set in the whole world." ■

> *In everything give thanks; for this is the will of God in Christ Jesus for you.*
> — 1 Thessalonians 5:18, NKJV

Almost Perfect Picture

Just before the bell rang, Mrs. Williams asked her sixth-grade class to settle down, put their books away, and listen carefully because she had a very important announcement to make. Angela quickly put her papers in her desk, stuffed her homework in her backpack, and waited for her teacher to continue.

"There's going to be a county-wide bookmark picture contest for all middle-school students. The theme is 'Inspire Others to Read.' On your picture, you are to write a slogan about why reading is important and then draw an illustration with a black marker pen. You will be judged for your creativity and originality. The winner will have his or her drawing printed on bookmarks, which will be given away throughout the county. I want all of you to enter this contest. It will be a big honor to win. Work on your picture at home and bring it to class in two weeks. I'll send them to the judges. Good luck."

Angela was excited as she burst through

Almost Perfect Picture

the door, "Mom! Mom! There's a picture contest about reading. It sounds fun. Maybe I'll even win."

"Remember, darling, doing your best is what's really important—not just the winning."

"I know, I know. But I love to draw and my teacher says I'm good at it. And I already know what I'm going to draw. It's going to be so cool."

"That's great. You can start on it just as soon as you practice your piano and finish your homework."

Angela dropped her backpack in the entryway and took her empty lunchbox to the kitchen. She then sat down at the piano. Thirty minutes dragged by. As soon as the clock said 4:30, she grabbed her backpack, found her history book, and started reading her assignment. It was tough concentrating on Civil War battles when her mind was racing with ideas about what she was going to draw—a spaceship, the moon, stars. She was going to try her best to win that contest.

As soon as her homework was done, Angela got out some paper, picked up a pencil, and began designing her picture. She first made a light sketch on the paper so she could erase any mistakes. All evening she worked to get the design just right. Across the bottom, she wrote, "Let Reading Take You Places." Then she drew the surface of the moon with a boy standing, reading a book. She made craters in the moon, a rocket ship in the background, and all kinds of stars and planets in the sky.

"Time for bed, darling," Mom said as she glanced at Angela's picture. "You've really been working hard on this. What a great idea about the moon! But it's time to put it away. Tomorrow is another day."

Reluctantly, Angela put down her pencil, took one last admiring look at her picture, and went to brush her teeth.

The next day, as soon as she got home from school and did her chores,

Almost Perfect Picture

Angela went back to her picture. She erased one of the stars which didn't look quite right and added some details to the boy's clothing and the rocket ship. At last, she was ready to start going over the pencil lines with a black marker pen. But that would have to wait, since once again it was bedtime.

As Mom was tucking Angela into bed, Mom said, "Leanne's mother mentioned that Leanne wants to come over tomorrow and spend some time with you." As Angela drifted off to sleep, she thought of all the fun things that she and Leanne could do together the next day. *The first thing I'll do,* Angela decided, *is show Leanne my picture.* Since Angela was an only child, having a teenage cousin was really special. Leanne was so talented and fun to be with. *Someday,* thought Angela, *when I'm in high school, I want to be just like Leanne.*

The next day, when Leanne came over, Angela could hardly wait to show her the picture she was drawing for the contest. "Wow, great job!" Leanne said, "I love what you've done, but I have a couple ideas of how it could be even better. Let me help you." Leanne paused, "You don't mind, do you?"

"Well, no, I want it to be really, really good. What do you think I should change?" Angela asked, thinking that Leanne would tell her a few ways to improve the drawing and then let Angela do it.

Instead, Leanne grabbed another sheet of paper and said, "Here let me show you how," as she began sketching her own ideas of what the drawing should look like.

"But, it's my picture—I need to draw it," Angela said.

"Don't worry," Leanne assured her, "It's your idea. Let me just finish the rocket ship and then you can draw a planet right here," Leanne said, pointing to a corner of the picture.

Almost Perfect Picture

Before Angela knew it, she was helping Leanne with the picture, instead of Leanne helping her. But when it was finished, it was a great drawing. In fact, it was much better than the one Angela had done by herself. There was only one problem— it wasn't really Angela's picture anymore. It was Leanne's *and* Angela's. And this was a middle-school contest, *not* a high school contest!

After Leanne went home, Angela looked at the picture. It was perfect. Leanne was a talented artist. *But,* Angela thought, *what should I do? It's more Leanne's than mine. Should I finish my first drawing and turn it in, or should I turn in this one?* No one, not even Angela's mom, knew how much Leanne had done on the picture. And if Angela didn't turn in Leanne's picture, would it hurt Leanne's feelings? After all, Leanne was only trying to be helpful. Angela didn't want Leanne to think that she didn't appreciate her help. Angela sighed. *I don't have to decide right now,* she thought, *I still have a week or so before the deadline.*

The days rushed by and Angela never found time to finish her original drawing. Besides, the picture she had drawn with Leanne was Angela's idea. She was the one who had written the slogan on the bottom of the picture. And Mrs. Williams had never said you couldn't have someone help you with the picture. So when the deadline arrived, Angela turned in the perfect picture.

Weeks went by and Angela had almost forgotten about the contest. Then one day, Mrs. Williams said, "Class, I have a very important announcement to make. I have just received a large envelope from the judges of the bookmark picture contest. Here's what the official letter says, 'Congratulations to Angela Wilson, the winner of this year's Bookmark Picture Contest.' Enclosed are bookmarks with Angela's drawing on

Almost Perfect Picture

them. There are enough for each student in the class to have one. There is also an envelope for Angela. It has a special award certificate in it and bookmarks for Angela to give to all of her family and friends."

Angela was shocked. Leanne's picture had won the contest.

Her classmates started clapping. "Way to go, Angela. You're a winner. Hip, hip, hooray!" Angela was too embarrassed to say anything while Mrs. Williams passed out the bookmarks to all the students. This was the first time they had seen the picture she had turned in.

Carolyn leaned over to Angela and said, "I knew you were good at drawing, but I didn't know you were this good!"

"Yeah!" Peter exclaimed. "You didn't do it by yourself, did you?"

Angela looked down and stammered, "It was my idea—and I worked hard on it."

Rachel shook her head, "I've never seen you draw this good before. Show us how you did it."

Doug handed her a paper and pencil. "Draw it again for us, Angela," he challenged.

What was she going to do? Just as she was about to draw the shape of the moon, the bell rang. "Don't forget that your book reports are due tomorrow," Mrs. Williams announced as everyone rushed out of the classroom.

"Saved by the bell," someone might say—but not really! Although Angela never had to admit to her friends that her cousin had helped her with the prize-winning picture, she no longer loved to draw. In fact, she avoided drawing pictures, especially in

Almost Perfect Picture

school. She was afraid that her friends would find out that she really couldn't draw as good as the picture that won the contest. And since she quit practicing, Angela never got any better at drawing than she was in sixth grade—all because of the secret behind the "almost" perfect picture. ■

> *Better to have little, with godliness, than to be rich and dishonest.*
> —Proverbs 16:8, NLT

Living Like Tahili

Nathan read the brochure in his hand again, letting the words and pictures sink in. It had come in the mail, along with catalogs advertising the latest computer games, *must-have* clothes for the season, and a range of new bikes that made Nathan's mouth water. He really wanted a new mountain bike with front suspension so he could fly down the hills with his friends. A small, folded brochure fell from the pile onto the floor. He picked it up, ready to throw it in the trash, when something caught his eye. A young child with sad eyes stared back at him from the page. It was obvious the child was sick or hungry. It turned out she was both.

Nathan opened the brochure and read all about Tahili, a five-year-old girl who lived in South Africa. Her father died in an accident when she was just a baby, and her mother had recently died too. Tahili was an orphan, being cared for by her elderly grandmother, who was too old to work in the fields and earn money. That

Living Like Tahili

meant there was no food for either of them. The brochure was asking people to help raise money to support orphans like Tahili.

As he lay in bed that night, trying to sleep, Nathan couldn't get the picture of Tahili's sad eyes out of his head. He thought back to one of the Bible verses he had learned last year: "Whatever you do for the least of these, you do for Me." Nathan loved God and talked to Him all the time. He wanted to be like King David and grow up to be a man after God's own heart. Was helping Tahili part of that? Nathan lay awake thinking of Tahili and her situation, long after the rest of the family was asleep. He was just a kid. What could he do?

By morning, he'd come up with a plan. Over breakfast he discussed it with his mom and dad. He would organize a fund-raiser for Tahili.

After school that day, instead of hanging out with his friends, he gave them a wave and headed for home. He let himself into the house, grabbed a bite to eat, sat at the computer, and began designing his own flyer.

As he typed, Nathan felt excitement growing inside him. It was even more of a rush than flying down the rocky hill behind his house on his mountain bike. He double-checked to make sure he hadn't made any spelling mistakes and pressed print. Fifty copies should be just right.

The next day, Nathan handed out the flyers to everyone he came across. He put a notice in the church newsletter and even asked the pastor if he could have a few minutes to present his idea to the church before the worship service began. Pretty soon, everybody knew about Tahili and what Nathan was planning to do. He would spend the next weekend living like Tahili!

When Nathan's fund-raiser finally arrived, Nathan ate his Friday night supper slowly, savoring each bite, but his stomach churned, knowing this

Living Like Tahili

was going to be his last meal until Sunday evening. To raise awareness of Tahili and her situation, Nathan was going without food for forty hours and people were sponsoring him for his effort. Every hour he went without food raised more money for Tahili. He wondered what it would feel like to be hungry. He was about to find out.

But that wasn't all Nathan had decided to do. After researching where Tahili and her grandmother lived, he discovered that they had no electricity, no running water, and slept on a dirt floor with just a blanket. Tahili didn't even have a pillow. Her grandmother had an old bike that she pedaled around the town and Tahili sat on the handlebars. There were no telephones, TVs, or computers in their village. Nathan wasn't just going to go without food for the weekend to help Tahili, he was also going to go without all of the modern conveniences that he lived with. He was

going to sleep outside on the grass in the backyard, would not use the phone or watch television, and he was going to ride his bike to church instead of going in the car. He wasn't even going to have a shower. For forty hours, his life was going to be as close to Tahili's as possible.

Nathan didn't get much sleep the first night. He tossed and turned, trying to find a comfortable spot on the hard ground in his backyard. With only a blanket, he got cold in the middle of the night and had to run around the house a few times to warm up. He also missed his pillow. His arm went to sleep whenever he rested his head on it for too long.

While the rest of the family drove to church in their car, Nathan and his dad rode their bikes. The church was farther away than Nathan had remembered and pedaling was a whole lot harder on an empty stomach.

Living Like Tahili

There was a special luncheon on that day; everyone was to enjoy a meal together after church. Nathan could smell the aroma of food baking in the ovens. He couldn't take his eyes off the macaroni and cheese, baked beans, and the yummy desserts that were just waiting to be eaten. But Nathan knew he wouldn't taste any of the food that was there. Instead, he sat in a chair, holding a sign. The sign read,

I'm raising money for a little girl in Africa named Tahili. For forty hours I'm living as closely as possible to the way Tahili lives. I'm not eating. I'm sleeping outside on the grass and I've given up all modern appliances like cell phones and TV. I even rode my bike to church instead of going in the car. All donations are gratefully received.

People ate and laughed and talked together over their big plates of food. Nathan sat holding his sign, his mouth watering like a summertime sprinkler. Occasionally, people came over and gave him money. When the luncheon was over, Nathan gave the money to his mom and got back on his bike for the long ride home.

In total, Nathan raised almost one thousand dollars for little Tahili and her grandmother. As he deposited the money into the bank a few days later, his stomach now full of breakfast and his skin nice and clean from a warm shower, he felt a rush of warmth spread over him. It felt good to help someone in need. It felt good to make a difference. Even though he was just a kid himself, Nathan's compassion for a child he'd never

Living Like Tahili

met would help change her life. He knew that one thousand dollars was enough to sink a well in the center of Tahili's village, so her entire community would have water close by, or buy enough grain to last Tahili and her grandmother through the winter, or pay for Tahili to go to the local school for more than a year. Best of all, he knew that whatever he had done for Tahili, he had actually done for Jesus. ■

> *Assuredly, I say to you, inasmuch as you did it to one of the least of these My brethren, you did it to Me.*
> —Matthew 25:40, NKJV

Snakes Alive

It was the first day of spring. Brilliant beams of sunlight glistened across the pond at the bottom of the hill, making the ground warm and melting away the last of winter's snow. The world was alive with the songs of birds and the buzz of insects enjoying the warmth and the promise of good weather. But birds and insects weren't the only things that were waking up!

On this particular day, Linda Kay and her friend, Tara, were having a good time playing together. But they soon tired of playing games inside the house and asked if they could play outside.

"Sure," Mom said, "you can play on the hill, but just don't go too close to the pond. There's lots of mud around the edge, and you could slip and fall into the water."

Linda Kay and her friends loved to play down by the pond, regardless of the season. In the summer, they would make rafts and float them on the water.

The pond in the winter, right before the spring thaw.

MISS BRENDA'S BEDTIME STORIES — VOLUME 1   89

Snakes Alive

In autumn, they'd collect brightly colored leaves from the trees that grew on the banks of the pond. In the winter, they would ice skate or just play slip and slide in their snow boots.

Mom liked to be outside where she could watch to make certain the children were safe and hear them if they called. But today she was very busy and had lots of housework to do. After dusting the furniture, Mom began vacuuming. Suddenly, she had the strangest feeling that she should turn off the vacuum. Why? She wasn't finished with the carpet. But she turned it off and looked around. She listened for a few moments, but not hearing anything, she started vacuuming again.

There it was again—that strong impression to turn off the vacuum. *Something isn't right,* she thought. *Maybe I should check on the girls.*

She opened the back door and walked out in the yard where she could see down the hill to the pond. From way down below, she heard, "Help! Mom! Help!" followed by the most blood-curdling scream!

Panic gripped her heart. She cupped her hands around her mouth and yelled, "Linda Kay! What's the matter?"

"Snakes!" came back the terrified reply. "Snakes! They're everywhere! Hurry! Please, Mom, hurry!"

Now anyone who knew Linda Kay's mom knew that she was absolutely petrified of snakes. But a mother will do almost anything to protect her child, even when it involves battling scary things.

Mom ran into the house and looked around for a weapon. The only thing she could find was a broom. Grabbing it, she ran as fast as she could down the hill. The girls' screams got louder the closer she got to them.

Suddenly, she screeched to a stop and gasped. Directly in front of her was a great big, monstrous black snake slowly slithering along

Snakes Alive

the pathway. Overcome with fear, she gulped, hardly able to swallow. Frantically, she scanned the area for a way around the snake. She had to rescue her daughter and her friend, Tara. But each time she tried a new path, another snake appeared. The panic-stricken girls wailed for help. She had to get to them and quickly!

With no way around the slithering creature, Mom poked at it with the bristles of the broom. Not appreciating her prodding, it slowly moved off the path. She raced a few more steps only to encounter another snake. Terrified, Mom prodded the second snake with her broom. And then there was a third snake, and a fourth. Snake by snake, she prodded and poked the creatures off the pathway and into the woods until she reached the girls. Sobbing, the frightened girls grabbed her, holding on for dear life!

Trembling like a leaf on a tree, Linda Kay cried, "Oh, Mom! What are we going to do? There are snakes everywhere!"

Sure enough, when Mom paused to assess their situation, she could hardly believe her eyes. Circled around them were what seemed like hundreds of snakes. She had no idea what kind they were or whether or not they were poisonous. All she knew was that they were big and black and they could be dangerous!

Linda Kay Walsh is thankful Jesus answered her prayer.

Breathless with fright, Mom prayed, "Oh, dear Jesus, please help me be brave. Help us to reach the house safely."

Mom instructed the girls to stay close to her even though she knew they had no thought of doing otherwise. Together, they inched their way up the hill. Whenever they encountered a snake, Mom would gently nudge it with her broom until it crawled off the pathway. Finally, exhausted from fear, they reached the safety of the house.

Snakes Alive

"I'm so glad you came and saved us from the snakes," Linda Kay said, as her mom tucked her into bed that night. "We were screaming and screaming but we couldn't get your attention. I was so scared. But I know why you finally heard us. I prayed and asked Jesus to help you hear us. And right then you came to the top of the hill. When I saw you, I knew Jesus answered my prayer."

Mom agreed, "With all the windows shut and the vacuum on, I would never have heard your screams. I'm sure it was God who impressed me to stop my vacuuming and go outside to listen."

Linda Kay's eyes sparkled with excitement. "I'm glad Jesus hears us when we pray. Mom, we need to thank Jesus again, because He kinda worked a miracle for us, didn't He?"

"Yes, sweetie," Mom agreed. "He sure did! It reminds me of a chapter in the Bible that my dad used to read to me when I was a little girl—especially when I was scared. Psalms ninety-one says that God will protect us from all kinds of things—even very poisonous snakes. I memorized the promise in verse eleven: 'For He shall give His angels charge over you, to keep you in all your ways.'"

"I'm going to memorize that too, just in case I ever meet up with a bunch of snakes again!" Linda Kay exclaimed.

A few days later, Mom was talking with their next door neighbor who had lived on that hill his entire life. She told him about meeting up with all the snakes down by the pond. "What I can't understand is that we've gone to the pond lots of times and seen an occasional snake, but never have we seen so many."

Judge Salmon explained, "There have always been lots of snakes on this hill—especially down by the pond. They hibernate during the winter,

Snakes Alive

but every year on the first warm day of spring, they come out to soak up the warmth of the sun. Then as the days get warmer, they crawl away and hide in their holes so you seldom see them. Fortunately for you, they are sluggish and move very slowly when they first waken."

Then he added, smiling, "They aren't poisonous, but they can sure give you a good scare—and a pretty mean bite." ■

> *My help comes from the LORD,*
> *Who made heaven and earth.*
> —Psalm 121:2, NKJV

Ice Queen

"Honey? Have you shoveled the driveway yet?" asked Mrs. Parker.

"Ugh," groaned Chrissy as she stood in front of the entryway mirror, adjusting her new winter hat. "Can't you leave me alone for just a few minutes to make sure I look decent before I go out and do slave labor!" She went back to making her adjustments.

"Chrissy," her mom replied impatiently, "you have had ten minutes. Now get it in gear and shovel that snow. And it's not slave labor, the rest of us clean up after you, cook your meals, and buy you those clothes that are preventing you from doing your chores. Now move!"

Chrissy pouted. *No one appreciates my beauty. When I was a baby, people fawned over me. But, I'm fourteen now and look at me! I could be a supermodel. I don't understand why people give me such a hard time. They must be jealous. My parents are old*

Ice Queen

and wrinkly, but my gorgeous auburn-brown hair falls just perfectly down around my shoulders, my complexion is flawless, and I have this adorable new winter outfit that makes me look absolutely fabulous. It's up to me to represent the family.

"Chrissy!" her mom called from the top of the stairs. She was standing there, tapping her foot. *"Now!"* she ordered, pointing her finger towards the door.

"Fine!" Chrissy shouted back. "But if everyone in this neighborhood thinks we are a bunch of homeless people who have taken residence in someone else's house because you didn't let me fix my hat, then I will not be held responsible!" She snatched her mittens off the entryway table, exited the door, and slammed it behind her. Mrs. Parker massaged her temples. "Oh, I feel a headache coming on," she sighed.

Once outside, Chrissy shuddered under the wicked January wind that whistled through the street. Then she let out a groan at the sight of four-foot-high drifts partially covering the car. Her dad had to work in his basement office today because he couldn't get the car out of the driveway.

She grabbed the shovel off the porch and set to work. She saw several other neighbors working hard to clear their driveways. Some were helping each other, sharing snowblowers and shovels to make the job easier. *Maybe one of them will see how cute I am and come help me. They'll think that I have mean parents. Seriously, who makes their delicate daughter come out and work in this weather?*

She saw Mr. Wellington. His family had just moved next door. They were a nice couple with two older kids. *Why, he certainly wouldn't make*

Ice Queen

his children shovel. I bet he never made them work like slaves! She was just about to call for help when the door of her next door neighbors on the other side opened. *Oh no . . .*

Out stepped Brett Dilbertson—the biggest loser she knew. For one, he did not dress to impress. There he stood in an atrocious pair of overalls and the dorkiest fur hat on his head. He had a dumb grin on his face and held a bright red shovel that matched the hideous red handkerchief around his neck. Quickly, Chrissy turned her back, pretending not see him. Too late.

"Hey there, Miss Chrissy!" he called. *Ugh, I don't want to talk to that loser. I'll pretend I didn't hear him; maybe he will go back inside his house.* Brett was an extremely nice boy, but when it came to reading the social cues of his peers, he was somewhat clueless. He lumbered down the icy stairs leading from his house into her yard, and then made his way up behind her. He gave her a hearty tap on the back.

"Chrissy!" he shouted with delight. She bristled, put on a fake smile, and turned around to converse with Brett, whom she considered to be a lesser life form.

"Hello, Brett," she said icily. "What are you doing out here?"

He laughed idiotically, throwing his head back. "I've come to help you, silly! I saw you from the window—"

"You've been watching me?" she said, horrified. Brett, realizing what his statement might have sounded like, began to backtrack.

"Uh, no, no. I mean I looked outside to see the weather and I saw you by accident and I thought I'd just come to help." This was *partially true*, and it was also *partially true* he was motivated to help because he thought Chrissy was the prettiest girl he knew. Chrissy knew this and had to think

Ice Queen

fast to get out of what would be at least an hour of work and being seen publicly with this embarrassing misfit!

"Well, that's very sweet," she replied. Brett's grin went ear to ear. "But," continued Chrissy, "that won't be necessary. You see, I like shoveling, it's kind of therapeutic, you know? It's fun—my favorite." Brett was baffled.

"You . . . like shoveling?" Brett said, his smile fading into a puzzled expression. Chrissy nodded. "But it's twenty degrees outside—"

"It sure is, isn't it invigorating?"

"It's freezing," Brett said, confused.

"Maybe for some people, but not for me. Now if you'll kindly excuse me, I would like to get back to work now." Brett smiled weakly and walked back toward his house, dragging the shovel behind him.

Whew! THAT was close. Now that he is inside, I'll see if I can get some real help from someone who won't embarrass me.

"Excuse me," she called to Mr. Wellington. He smiled and walked over.

"Hi, Chrissy, what can I do for you?" he asked.

"Well, my parents have asked me to shovel this mess all by myself. And it's not like I don't want to do my share, but as you can see I'm not the manual-labor type." Mr. Wellington nodded, looking deep in thought.

"So the thing is, sir, I was hoping that you might be able to help me shovel." She opened her eyes wide and smiled sweetly. Mr. Wellington continued with his thoughtful expression for a moment, then smiled, placing a hand on her shoulder.

"Well, Chrissy, the thing is, I have it from a very reliable source that

Ice Queen

you enjoy shoveling snow." Chrissy's smile disappeared. Mr. Wellington continued, "I have even heard some people find it quite therapeutic." Chrissy began to panic.

"But it feels like zero degrees out here!" she protested. Mr. Wellington just laughed.

"It's not cold, it's refreshing," he said as he turned and walked the few steps back to his house. She watched in disbelief as he put his shovel away and went inside.

After a few more moments of standing in shock—not only because he had heard what she told Brett, but because she actually got a sense of what she must have sounded like—she thought she might give Brett another chance. But as she turned around, she saw their garage door open and Brett, along with his family, back out in their old pickup truck. He waved to her and shouted, "Have fun!" out the window. They had sleds piled up in the bed of the truck, and she could only guess at the fun they were about to have as she would now have to shovel the snow alone.

It took Chrissy much longer than she could have possibly imagined to

finish shoveling. Her fingers were so cold she could hardly manage to unzip her warm winter jacket as she kicked off her boots at the same time. She was still grumbling under her breath about having to work that hard when she heard Dad calling, "Chrissy, is that you? Have you finished shoveling?"

"Yes, it's all done! But I'm absolutely mortified at how many people drove by and saw me working like a slave! I'll never hear the end of it at school tomorrow!" she answered with a disgusted tone. "I need to talk to you in my office. Can you come right now please?" Dad asked in a firm voice.

Ice Queen

"What do you want now?" Chrissy flopped down in the chair in front of Dad's desk. Dad looked rather serious, which made her a bit uneasy. "Chrissy, I just got off the phone with Mr. Wellington, and I know all about your conversation with Brett—" "But Dad—" Chrissy interrupted. Dad put his hand up and motioned for her to be still. "I want you to listen to me. You seem to think that you are better than everyone else. But the Bible says that God created us to be equals. No one is better than anyone else. Somehow that is a lesson that you have not yet learned. Mom and I made some decisions while you were out shoveling. Brett and his family help out at the homeless shelter every Sunday afternoon, and for the rest of the year, you will be joining them."

"What! You can't possibly mean . . ." Chrissy protested, but Mom interrupted as she walked in the door and sat down next to Chrissy. "Yes, Dad is right. You not only will help them at the shelter, but you will ride with them each week as well." Chrissy began to cry, pleading with her parents to change their minds. But they stood firm in their decision. At the end of the year, Chrissy was a different girl. She wasn't proud, selfish, or conceited! She became someone everyone loved—because now she was always thinking of others! She had finally learned the valuable lesson to esteem others better than herself! ∎

> *Let nothing be done through selfish ambition or conceit, but in lowliness of mind let each esteem others better than himself.*
> —Philippians 2:3, NKJV

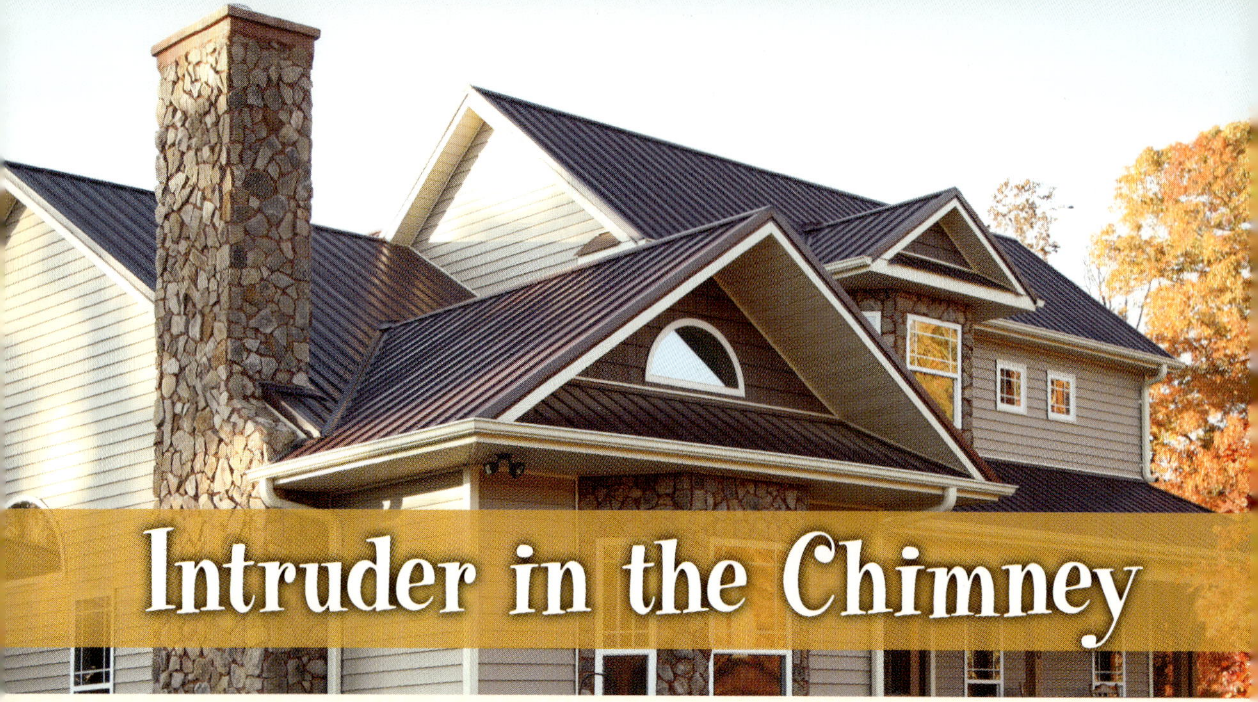

Intruder in the Chimney

The sun had barely peeked above the horizon when Penny, a border collie, pranced back and forth on the deck beside the kitchen. Her shrill bark announced her displeasure at still being outside instead of inside with her family. Intent on attracting their attention, Penny ignored Bella, the family's gray and white cat, who kept darting between her legs.

"Cassie," Mom called from her bedroom, "would you please let that dog inside the house before she wakes the entire neighborhood?"

"Sure, Mom." Half asleep, Cassie ambled to the kitchen. "Be quiet, Penny. I'm coming! I'm coming!" As Cassie opened the sliding-glass door, the animals tripped over one another to be the first to charge into the kitchen. Penny greeted Cassie with yips, leaps, and slobbery kisses, while Bella dashed straight for her food dish. After making sure Cassie felt duly appreciated, the dog ran to greet the other members of the family.

Cassie yawned. She opened the

Intruder in the Chimney

refrigerator and poured herself a glass of orange juice. As she sat at the table drinking her juice, she heard a strange noise. It sounded kind of creepy, like something scratching on the inside of a metal barrel.

As quickly as the scratching started, it stopped. Cassie put down her glass and listened more intently. Seconds later, the scratching sound returned. It seemed to be coming from the living room. When she got up from the table to follow the noise, it stopped. Standing silently in the middle of the living room, Cassie waited for the scratching to begin again.

She didn't have to wait long. There it was! *Scratch, scratch, scratch,* coming from the fireplace! Her eyes opened wide; her heart pounded faster. Something was stuck in the chimney! Living in a small country town in Oregon, she knew it could be almost anything—a squirrel, a bird, a rat, a raccoon, a skunk, or maybe even a groundhog. She hated groundhogs!

"Dad! Mom!" Cassie screamed and ran down the hallway toward her parents' bedroom. "Something's caught in the chimney! Hurry! Hurry!"

The bedroom door flew open. Penny bounded down the hallway, barking excitedly.

"Something's in the chimney. Come quick!"

"How do you know?" Mom grabbed her bathrobe, putting her arms in the sleeves as she ran toward the living room.

"Tell Dad we need him!" Cassie's voice came in short, frightened gasps. On one hand, she felt sorry for the trapped creature, but on the other hand, she was terrified that it might bite her. Bella, who was always serene and queenly, lay on the back of the sofa, observing the action from a safe distance.

"Dad's in the shower. He'll be out in a few minutes," Mom said breathlessly.

Intruder in the Chimney

"Don't get too close to the chimney," Cassie warned her. "Whatever is in there might bite."

Penny's excited barking at the fireplace opening had silenced the intruder in the chimney.

"Penny, be quiet! I need to listen." Mom grabbed the poker from the holder beside the fireplace, stooped over, and bravely rattled it back and forth inside the chimney. *Bang! Bang! Bang!* Black soot fell and covered her head. Mom coughed and stood up. Penny's shrill barking and frantic leaping about the hearth made it difficult for Mom to think. "Penny! Go lay down!" she ordered.

Mom returned the poker to its stand and brushed a lock of hair from her forehead. When she turned around, Cassie laughed. "Oh, Mom, your hair is covered with soot and you have a streak of black across your forehead and some on the tip of your nose. You look so funny." Cassie laughed even louder.

"Stop laughing. It's not funny," Mom said, although she couldn't help but laugh herself.

"Oh my! I'm a mess!" Mom looked at her hands, and then rolled her eyes toward the ceiling. "I'd better wash up before I get soot on my robe. Dad," she called as she headed for the hall bathroom, "we need you."

"So what's the big emergency?" asked Dad, still drying his hair with a towel as he hurried into the room.

Amid Penny's barking, Cassie explained about the scratching she had heard coming from inside the chimney. "Penny! Go lay down!" Dad ordered. Penny was too excited to obey. Dad grabbed the poker and rattled it inside the chimney. *Bang! Bang! Bang!*

"Mom already tried that!" Cassie shouted over Penny's deafening bark.

Dad peered up into the dark chimney.

"Can you see anything?" Cassie asked.

"No. Get me the broom!" Dad took the excited dog to the far side of

Intruder in the Chimney

the living room. "Penny! *Sit!*" The last thing Penny wanted to do was sit, but this time she obeyed. "Now, *stay!*"

The dog looked pleadingly at Dad, who repeated his command, *"Stay!"* Once the dog stopped barking, the scratching began. This sparked Bella's interest in the inhabitant in the chimney. Bella perked up her ears, rose to her feet, stretched, and began pacing back and forth in front of the fireplace, emitting a low growl and chattering her teeth as if chanting, *"Lunch! Lunch! Lunch!"*

Cassie returned with the broom and handed it to her father. "Whatever it is, don't hurt it," she begged.

Dad put the bristle end of the broom up into the chimney and wiggled it around. "I'll try not to, honey, but the animal will die up there if we can't dislodge it."

Swoosh! Swoosh! Rattle! Rattle! Bang! Bang! He shoved the broom into the chimney as far as his arm could go. When his arm got tired, Dad withdrew the broom in a billow of soot. He'd barely moved away from the fireplace when a poof of squirming soot thudded to the hearth.

"It's a bird!" shouted Cassie. Dad reached for the creature. The terrified bird shook himself, slapped the air with his wings, and flew toward the ceiling in a cloud of soot. A long black feather from the bird's left wing drifted to the floor.

This was too much for even a border collie's self-control, and Penny bounded across the room, barking frantically at the strange intruder.

"Quick! Open the sliding door!" Dad shouted, using the broom to coax the bird toward freedom. Instead, the terrified creature spotted the world beyond the giant picture window and flew full force into the glass. Stunned, the bird dropped to the windowsill.

Intruder in the Chimney

With Penny barking and running in circles in the middle of the room, Bella sprang into action. Intent on a little "fast food," the cat leaped from the floor to the back of the chair to the windowsill.

"No, Bella! No!" Cassie grabbed for the cat, while Dad reached for the bird.

Mom appeared just in time for the suddenly conscious bird to fly up into the air, across the room, and plop right on top of her head.

"Eeeeeeek!" Mom screamed and danced about the room, trying to dislodge the creature from her hair. The yapping Penny ran frantic circles around her. Before Dad could come to Mom's rescue, the bird spotted the open door. With Penny and Bella charging after, the bird swooped to freedom.

The next morning when Cassie sat down at the kitchen table, a medium-sized black bird landed on the corner post and began to sing.

Curious, Cassie opened the sliding door. Instead of immediately flying away, the bird continued to sing. After a few minutes, the bird spread his wings and took off. "Hey, his left wing is missing a feather," Cassie exclaimed. "Could he be the bird that got stuck in our chimney yesterday?"

Mom, who was frying potatoes for breakfast, laughed, "I doubt it. After such a scare, that bird is probably in the next county by now."

No one would have thought more about it, except the next morning a black bird with a missing feather landed on the same deck post. After serenading the family for a few minutes, he flew away. All summer long, the same black bird arrived at approximately the same time each morning, sang his song and left. It was almost as if he was saying, "Thank you! Thank you!"

Intruder in the Chimney

If a bird can show his gratitude, how much more important it is for girls and boys—creatures made in God's image—to be thankful! ■

> *Giving thanks always for all things to God the Father in the name of our Lord Jesus Christ.*
> —Ephesians 5:20, NKJV

Help! Save Me!

Craig lay awake in his bed, thinking about dying. Recently, he'd faced death not once, but twice! The first time he had, in fact, "died." The second time, he had barely escaped.

How can a person die and then live to face death again? Craig did. Both events took place in water—lots of water—with his family watching.

Craig lived in St. Kitts, a beautiful island in the Caribbean Sea. His mother heard about some revival meetings being held in the northern part of the island and took her family. It was there that Craig decided to give his life to Jesus and be baptized.

So, on a warm, sunny afternoon, the preacher led Craig and his friends, who also wanted to be baptized, down to the beach and waded into the crystal clear water. As church members sang from the shore and his family waved encouragement, the preacher lowered Craig under the waves, signifying he was "dying" to a life of sin and being "born" to a new life with Jesus.

Help! Save Me!

That was death number one.

The very next day, Craig and his family decided to return to that same beach, but this time to fly kites and swim in the cool, clear Caribbean Sea. They arrived at the almost deserted stretch of sand just before eight o'clock in the morning and found a wonderful breeze blowing, perfect for kite flying. Craig easily launched his kite but before long, he became bored and announced he wanted to go for a swim. "Fine with me," said Dad, "I'll join you."

Troy, Craig's younger brother, called, "Me too!"

As Mother and Craig's older brother, Ryan, watched from the shore, Dad, Craig, and Troy waded out into the sea, enjoying the refreshing water and the tug and pull of the waves. Each could swim and each felt perfectly safe, right up to the moment Dad disappeared.

It happened suddenly, without any warning. Craig's father simply vanished below the waves, as if the ocean had swallowed him whole. The two boys froze where they were, unsure of what was going on.

With a splash, their father resurfaced and breathlessly shouted, "Stay where you are!"

Craig was about to call out, "What's happening?" but only got out the word *what* before it felt as if someone pulled the sandy bottom out from under him. As he struggled toward his father, he found that his feet could no longer touch the bottom.

Hey, I'm a good swimmer, he thought to himself. *This isn't a problem. I'll just head back to shore.* But when he started to swim, a sickening realization hit him. He wasn't getting anywhere. In fact, he found himself struggling with all his might just to stay above the surface of the sea.

Help! Save Me!

Some force was pulling him down, dragging him under the waves!

That's when Craig noticed that the water around him was beginning to spin. He couldn't believe his eyes. He'd heard others talk about dangerous whirlpools in the sea, but he had never experienced one himself. The awful truth was that he was being pulled into a strong, fast-moving whirlpool. And so was his dad.

Fear seized him as he found himself forced under water by the tremendous sucking action created by the whirlpool. Craig's leisurely swim had become a struggle for survival.

At one point he returned to the surface and heard his father screaming to his little brother. "Get back to the beach!"

As Craig began to sink again, he reached out and grabbed his father's neck and, together, they vanished below the waves. Everything was spinning around and around. When Dad's feet finally hit the sand, it jerked Craig so violently that he lost hold of his dad. Opening his eyes, he saw his father being dragged away by the current. But his dad managed to reach out and take hold of Craig's arm and hold on with all his might. The two were swept back and forth, up and down, and around and around by the powerful currents.

A cold chill went through Craig's body as he struggled against the powerful swirl of the water. *This is it*, he thought to himself. *I'm going to die right here and now. But I don't want to die! I want to live!*

That's when he remembered the words of the pastor who'd been teaching him about Jesus before his baptism. "God is always listening to His children; always ready to help in times of trouble." *Can it be that right now, Jesus is listening to me; even here, under the violently swirling*

Help! Save Me!

waters? Jesus, Craig called out in his mind, *help! Save me! I need You. Help me and my dad. Please. Help us!* Suddenly, Craig wasn't afraid anymore. He knew Jesus was with him and could save him.

While Craig was praying, his mother was running down the beach toward her older son, shouting, "Ryan, Ryan! Dad and Craig are in trouble. Help them! Please help them!"

Ryan took one look and realized his dad and brother were being sucked under the waves. He quickly raced toward the water. He was a strong, experienced swimmer and had learned how to judge the ocean's currents. He knew just how to approach the area where his father and brother were struggling; he could—maybe—help them escape the swirling water. He also knew that God could give him the strength he needed to save his brother and dad. He wouldn't be swimming alone. His heavenly Father would be with him, showing him the way to go and keeping him safe.

When he reached the spot where he'd last seen Craig and his dad, he slipped under the surface of the water and quickly located the thrashing pair. Tearing Craig from his father's neck, he began fighting the currents, moving slowly toward the surface and the shore. His father, freed from the weight of his thrashing son, finally surfaced and took in great gasps of air as he struggled to free himself from the spinning water.

After Ryan deposited a coughing, sputtering Craig on the beach, he quickly returned to help his father fight his way to shore.

"I still get chills thinking about that day," Craig tells his friends each time he relates his story. "I almost died a second time on the very same beach. My first death—my baptism—had been filled with singing and smiles. My second death would have been filled with shouting and

Help! Save Me!

tears. But I learned something before my baptism that helped me in the whirlpool and will help me if I ever face death again. You don't have to be afraid of dying with Jesus. When Jesus is with you, you can face anything. And no matter what, God hears you when you call for help." Craig always concludes his story by saying, "I'm so thankful that the first death I experienced taught me how to face the second." ■

> *Turn your ear to me, come quickly to my rescue;*
> *Be my rock of refuge, a strong fortress to save me.*
> —Psalm 31:2, NIV

The Forbidden Concert

Jen came running up to Krista in the school hallway. "I've been looking all over for you. Where've you been all morning? I've got the most incredible news!"

"What's happening? Is your mom going to let you go to camp this summer?"

"No, no, that's not it — she hasn't made up her mind yet. Besides, that's not until summer. What I wanted to tell you is happening next month."

"What's happening?"

"No, you gotta guess," teased Jen.

"Guess what?"

"Guess who's coming to El Paso?"

"Santa Claus!"

"No, silly. It's the Jones Brothers!"

"You've got to be kidding!" Krista gasped.

"No, I'm not. And my aunt is taking me to the concert and she said I could invite a friend. Wanna go?"

"Does a cat meow? Of course, I

MISS BRENDA'S BEDTIME STORIES — VOLUME 1   111

The Forbidden Concert

want to go!"

"She said she has third row tickets. Can you imagine? Front center seats. Can't get any better than that!"

"Yeah, you're right. But there's a slight problem. I don't think my parents approve of me going to teen concerts."

"You've got to be kidding! The Jones Brothers are good kids. Their dad used to be a pastor. Why would your parents be against them? I could understand if it were some wild rock group, but let's face it, these guys are clean—don't do drugs, don't smoke, don't drink—and they sing clean songs. Some even say their music is kinda like Christian rock."

"I know. I know. I think they're the greatest and I'm dying to see them. I even have a poster of them on the wall of my room—and I'm almost finished with a jacket I'm making that has Kyle's, John's, and Mark's pictures on it. It would be perfect to wear to the concert."

"So . . ."

"It's just that my parents have this thing against teen concerts. They say there's too much emotional mania and the crowds go berserk. They just don't think it's safe. Maybe when I'm older—but I can just hear them, 'Krista, you're only fourteen. That's no place for a fourteen-year-old!'"

"Do you think my aunt would take me if it weren't safe? Come on, you know the statistics. I'm sure more people die riding in cars than at rock concerts."

"You don't have to convince me. I'm in! I just don't know what I'm going to tell my parents."

"Why do you have to tell them anything? Just come over to my place

The Forbidden Concert

for a sleepover and your parents will never know."

"I'm not sure. I've never lied to my parents before."

"Well, you'll never get another offer like this. I'm giving you a chance of a lifetime to see your favorite musical group. But if you decide you can't go, I'm sure I could find dozens of girls who'd die for the chance." And with that, Jen turned around and headed off to her next class.

All the way home on the bus, Krista felt the weight of the world on her shoulders. What should she do? There was nothing wrong, she kept telling herself, in wanting to hear the Jones Brothers sing LIVE. Her mind was running in circles. *Should I tell my parents? Maybe they would let me? But if they say No, then that would be worse, because I would be disobeying!*

When Krista got home, she immediately went to her room and flopped down on her bed. *What should I do?* She decided to get out the Jones Brothers jacket she was working on. She put it on and admired it. She had cut out pictures of the boys from T-shirts and stitched them on to the front and back of her outfit. For her first sewing project, she thought it looked pretty good.

"Hey," Mom said as she walked past Krista's room, "that's a pretty neat jacket you've been working on. Are those the Jones Brothers?"

"Yes," said Krista, "they're the greatest."

"I noticed in the paper that they're coming to El Paso," Mom commented.

"Yes, they are. Is there any way that I could go? Jen is going and so are a lot of my other friends. Please?" Krista pleaded.

The Forbidden Concert

"You know we don't approve of teen concerts, honey." Mom placed a pile of folded laundry on her dresser. "It's almost time for bed. Is all of your homework done?"

Krista nodded and watched as Mom left the room. She knew it wouldn't do her any good to beg, but she was so disappointed.

The next day, Jen rushed up and asked, "Did you talk to your parents about the concert?"

"Well, sort of. At least I talked to my mom."

"Did she say you could go?"

"Well, she didn't say I couldn't—at least not in those words. Mom just said she didn't approve, but she didn't actually say I couldn't go," Krista reasoned.

"Great! This is going to be so cool. Just think! Third row seats at a Jones Brothers concert. Ta-da!"

"Do you think I could just spend the night at your house?"

"Sounds great to me. My mom's going to be gone that weekend—some seminar in Dallas—that's why my aunt is staying with me and taking us to the concert. Just count on it."

Krista got permission from her mom to have a sleepover at Jen's house that Saturday night. She packed her Jones Brothers jacket with her overnight stuff. When Mom dropped her off at Jen's house, she felt a pang of guilt, but quickly shrugged it off.

Mom and Dad will never know about the concert. And I really didn't lie anyway. I just didn't tell them everything. Besides what they don't know won't hurt them—or me. After all, this is a once in a lifetime opportunity. And maybe some of the songs will be what people call Christian rock. Or maybe they'll talk about helping others, like how they give money to help kids with diabetes. That's a good Christian thing to do.

The concert was everything Krista hoped it would be. She wasn't quite sure if any of the songs were Christian rock—they didn't sound like the songs she heard in church. And they didn't talk about helping others. But they seemed like really, really nice guys—and, wow, could they sing!

The Forbidden Concert

What was the most exciting for Krista was that everyone loved her Jones Brothers jacket. She got many compliments on it. One guy even asked her what her name was and how old she was. Then he asked if he could take her picture. "Did your parents bring you?" he inquired.

"No," she replied, "they didn't want me to come, so I had to sneak out of the house." All that attention really made her feel important.

The next morning, Krista woke up early. Jen's aunt had volunteered to give her a ride home and she didn't want to be late. While she was waiting, she thought about how her parents would feel if they found out what she had done. Her conscience was beginning to bother her. She didn't like keeping things from them and she was beginning to wish she hadn't lied. *But I did have such an awesome time, and as long as Mom and Dad don't find out, no harm done,* she reasoned.

Krista's mom and dad were just finishing up breakfast when she walked through the door. "How did the sleepover go?" they asked.

"Fine," she answered

"Did you have a good time?"

"Yes, thanks for letting me go," Krista replied.

Then she breathed a sigh of relief when they changed the subject. *So far, so good,* thought Krista.

"There are warm pancakes in the oven for you," Mom said, as Krista pushed the thick Sunday newspaper away from her place at the table and began to drink her orange juice.

Suddenly, Krista took a closer look at the top headline and the picture under it, "Jones Brothers Concert Wows El Paso Teens." Underneath was her picture with the caption, "Krista Harris, 14, in her Jones Brothers

The Forbidden Concert

jacket, said, 'My parents wouldn't let me go to the concert, so I had to sneak out of the house.'"

Krista immediately broke into tears and sobbed, "Mom, Dad, I'm so sorry!"

"Krista, we are very disappointed that you disobeyed us. We told you not to go to that concert. We trusted you. Did you really think we wouldn't find out?" Dad asked.

"I don't know. I just really wanted to go so bad, and I knew if I asked, you would say No! I guess I just got caught up in all the excitement, and I knew it would be so much fun. But it was wrong and I shouldn't have done it. I'm really sorry; will you forgive me?" Krista pleaded.

"Yes, of course we'll forgive you," Mom said. "However there are always consequences for your actions. We trusted you, and you broke that trust. It's going to take some time to rebuild it. There will be no more sleepovers or friends invited over for a month."

Krista felt so guilty that she didn't even protest the terms of punishment. She felt even worse the next day at school when all her friends laughed and teased her about the newspaper article. And if that wasn't bad enough, her principal called her into his office to let her know how disappointed he was in her.

Krista had a long talk with God and asked forgiveness for disobeying her parents and for breaking the ninth commandment, "Thou shalt not bear false witness." That weekend she learned a very important lesson, that honesty is always the best policy! ■

> *Be sure your sin will find you out.*
> —Numbers 32:23, NKJV

Forgotten Lunch

Sarah grabbed her backpack filled with books and homework, slung it over her shoulders, and headed out of the house. At the end of the block, she stopped to adjust her backpack when, all of a sudden, she realized she had forgotten her lunch. It was sitting on the kitchen counter in a brown paper bag. In her rush to get out the door, she'd forgotten to put it in her pack. She looked at her watch. If she hurried back home, she would still be on time to meet her friend, Melissa.

Sarah ran up the hill, opened the door, grabbed her lunch, and kissed her mom goodbye the second time. She hurried out the door and started back to school again.

Sarah walked to school most days. She enjoyed the cool, early morning air as she walked along Hobart Road with cars whizzing by. It took about twenty-five minutes to get to school, and for the first fifteen minutes, Sarah walked alone. She had to cross two small roads on the way and always took care to look

Forgotten Lunch

both ways before she crossed. On the second corner, she would meet up with Melissa. They would walk the rest of the way together, including crossing the overpass on a pedestrian bridge that went across busy Hobart Road.

Melissa and Sarah were both in sixth grade but were in different classrooms. Since they didn't see each other much during school, they enjoyed walking together. They would chatter and giggle and talk about school and friends and homework and boys. Sometimes they would stop in the middle of the overpass and watch the cars and trucks below.

Sarah knew she'd have to hurry if she wanted to meet up with Melissa. Forgetting her lunch made her later than usual, so she walked a little faster. As she crossed the first road, Sarah looked into the distance and saw Melissa waving at her. Sarah waved back, and Melissa motioned that she was going to keep walking. Neither girl liked being late for school, so Sarah understood. She would just hurry and try to catch up with Melissa farther along the way.

Sarah walked as quickly as she could, her backpack bouncing on her shoulders. She watched Melissa climb the stairs of the overpass, just like they always did together. As Sarah turned to watch the traffic on Hobart Road, she saw something that made her gasp. A big truck was rumbling up the main road. There

Forgotten Lunch

were always lots of trucks on Hobart Road, but this one was different. This one had its scoop bucket pointing straight up into the sky as it drove along, instead of down where it was supposed to be.

Sarah looked quickly from the truck to the overpass, then back to the truck again. The pedestrian bridge had been hit once before by a truck that was too tall to fit underneath, but it was during school and there was no one walking across. Seized with fear, Sarah realized that the truck was going to hit the bridge and Melissa had already climbed the stairs and was beginning to cross!

Sarah began to scream, "Melissa! Melissa! Get down!" She ran as fast as she could, waving her arms wildly, watching the truck get closer and closer to the overpass where her friend was walking. Sara screamed even louder! Melissa quickly turned around at the sound of Sarah's voice and saw the truck coming. But it was too late!

Although Melissa ran as fast as she could to get off the overpass, she only made it down one step before the truck's scoop bucket hit the bridge with a loud *crash*! Sarah stopped, tears streaming down her cheeks as she heard the ear-piercing sound of metal on metal and saw the overpass buckle in the middle. She watched helplessly as Melissa was thrown from the steps and onto the road below.

By the time Sarah got to the scene of the accident, all the traffic had stopped and people from nearby shops were hurrying to help. Melissa was lying very still on the road. Someone put a blanket over her to keep her warm. A kind lady hurried Sarah across the road and insisted she go on to school.

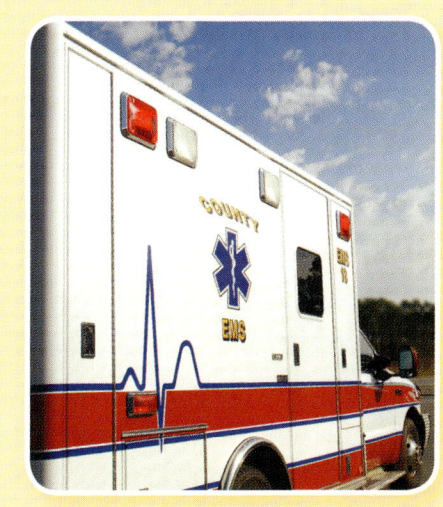

Sarah walked up the hill to school in a daze. If she hadn't forgotten her lunch, she would have been on the overpass too. The ambulance sirens

Forgotten Lunch

echoed in Sarah's head as she cried and walked the rest of the way to school.

When she arrived, Sarah went to the library to be with her favorite teacher, Mrs. Dunn, who also went to church with Sarah. Mrs. Dunn sat Sarah down and got her a glass of water and contacted Sarah's mother to let her know she was safe. Soon, news arrived that Melissa was alive, but she was badly injured and had to be taken to a larger hospital two hours away. She had a serious head injury from falling from the overpass.

At home that night, Sarah and her mom were talking when there was a knock at the door. It was a policeman. Sarah was one of the few people who actually saw what happened, and although she was only eleven years old, she was an important witness. The policeman sat down with Sarah and her mom

and wrote down all that Sarah remembered about the accident.

As he rose to leave, the policeman spoke quietly to Sarah's mother. Sarah tried to hear what he was saying, but couldn't. After the policeman left, Sarah's mom sat down and put her arms around her.

"The policeman had some bad news, honey," she said. "Melissa's injuries were very severe, and although the doctors did everything they could, the policeman just learned that Melissa died. He wanted to tell us himself so we didn't hear it on the news first."

Sarah started to cry again, and her mom held her close. "Mom, she can't be dead! She just can't be! Let's pray for her and her family—and for the doctors." Then Sarah, her mom, and her little brother knelt on the floor in the living room and prayed for a miracle for Melissa.

Forgotten Lunch

The next day, Sarah stayed home from school. She was still very shocked and sad by what had happened. In the middle of the morning, there was another knock at the door. It was the policeman again. This time, he was smiling. "I'm so sorry, but I got it wrong," he said. "Melissa is still very badly hurt and she's in the intensive care unit, but the doctors think she's going to pull through."

Sarah was smiling as she and her mom prayed again, but this time it was a prayer of thanks.

After eight long weeks in the hospital, Melissa was back at school again. Her only reminder of the accident was a little scar on her head. Once again, Sarah and Melissa enjoyed walking to school together, but every time they crossed the Hobart Road overpass, Sarah remembered the day she forgot her lunch!

If you make the LORD your refuge, . . . he will order his angels to protect you wherever you go.
—Psalm 91:9, 11, NLT

Devil's Tongue Temptation

The sunshine illuminated the lovely slopes of Harbor Hills on a bright January morning. Skiers of all ages and sizes cascaded down the runs. Most of them enjoyed exhilarating speeds as they glided over the surface of the snow on two pieces of fiberglass attached to their feet. However, for Thomas, the day was being wasted on the bunny hill.

The youth group at church had planned this skiing adventure a month ago and all were thrilled to go. Pastor Mike had been before, and he promised to teach everyone how to ski. Little did he realize, he had the most uncoordinated youth group in the nation. Everyone was stumbling, tumbling, and rolling down the hill. Everyone except Thomas.

Thomas took to the slopes naturally. He only stumbled once, but held his balance. The rest of his runs were flawless. But he grew bored and felt embarrassed at everyone's lack of ability. He watched them from the bottom of the bunny hill and then

Devil's Tongue Temptation

turned his gaze to the snowmakers spraying snow over far more stimulating runs.

"I need to get off this hill," he muttered, as he watched Samantha, a girl from church, fall and get caught on the towrope. She screamed and laughed as it dragged her back up to the top. He waited for Pastor Mike to finish his run. He noticed Thomas right away and called out to him as he made his way over.

"Hey there, Thomas," he said, removing his goggles and smiling. "Taking a little breather? You've really done well. I'm impressed!"

Thomas cleared his throat. "Yes, well, I would like to talk to you about that. I am far beyond this level of slope. And I wanted to let you know I am going down a different hill."

Pastor Mike wore a concerned expression. "Well, sure, I guess, Thomas. Which run did you have in mind?" he said, pulling out a map of Harbor Hills.

Great, thought Thomas. *He will make me go down some dumb green circle.*

Sure enough, Pastor Mike suggested several circles with names like Simple Slide and Ramblin' Run. All of which sounded incredibly boring. Thomas groaned.

"Really, sir? I mean, couldn't I take on a blue square? Or how about that one!" he said, pointing to a run called Devil's Tongue.

Pastor Mike shook his head. "No way, Thomas," he said. "That's a black diamond run. It's very steep and if you look from here you can see it, and not even experienced skiers are going down it. Please stay with the green circles." With that, he excused himself to go into the chalet to use the restroom.

It was now or never. Thomas turned to his friends who had just

Devil's Tongue Temptation

come down the hill and announced his intentions, "Attention my falling friends!" A collective groan emerged from the group as they gathered around Thomas. Thomas had a long history of being the best when it came to a lot of things. It's not that people minded him being talented; they just didn't like having him remind them all the time.

"As you may know," began Thomas in the pompous voice he used when giving speeches, "my skiing ability is far superior than yours! And while I shall miss all of you and your admirable attempts at skiing, I must venture forth."

Sally would have none of it. "So, what exactly are you trying to say?" she snapped. Then she smiled, "Do you get to go home early?" Everyone giggled. Thomas wasn't fazed.

"Laugh and joke if you must. But while you're on the bunny hill, I will be soaring down Devil's Tongue!" he said, pointing dramatically behind everyone. They all turned and beheld a vacant run that had one short steep dip followed by another that looked as though it went straight down.

"There's no way Pastor Mike will let you go down that thing," Sally said.

"He's not here to stop me," declared Thomas. And with that, he began making his way to the ski lift. Before they knew it, they were watching a laughing Thomas ride his way to the top. The lift took him higher than he expected, and he noticed a strange, queasy feeling whenever he looked down. *Must be the cold air,* he thought.

At the top, he exited the lift, but nearly got a ski caught. The lift was different from the tow rope. Nevertheless, he shook it off and glided towards a sign pointing in two directions. Toward the left was Ramblin' Run with a beautiful green circle next to it. Confidently,

Devil's Tongue Temptation

Thomas went right.

Those wimps at the bottom will be amazed at how fast I go. It only took a few moments to come to the edge of the run. The view was fantastic and, had Thomas been honest with himself, a little frightening. Down below he could see his friends; little specks all staring up at him. He also thought he saw Pastor Mike waving at him from one of the chairlifts. It was time to go. Taking a deep breath and tightening his grip on the ski poles, Thomas launched himself down the run.

For a few seconds, Thomas felt good about his decision. Then as he began to pick up speed, things went horrifyingly wrong. The run wasn't smooth. It was choppy and there were bumps. He managed to make it down the little steep hill but as the main drop approached, he felt sick.

The final drop was so steep that as he approached all he could see was the edge. It looked like he was heading toward a cliff—and fast. He swallowed hard and tried to snowplow to slow down; but he shot off the edge and flew briefly in the air. That's when he saw the bottom was almost straight down. He landed, and two things happened.

First, he realized he had forgotten to put his ski goggles on, and at the speed he was going his eyes began to water, making it difficult to see. Second, he realized that all the powdery snow was gone and he was sliding on glare ice. His skis were moving around beyond his control on the slick surface. *The run hasn't been groomed! It's all ice!*

Approaching speeds he never thought possible, it was only a matter of moments before things would come crashing to a stop. The moment came swiftly. His right ski glanced off the uneven surface and stuck vertically in another groove, spinning Thomas around and slamming him face-first into the icy hill. Skis and poles flew in all directions. When he came to a

Devil's Tongue Temptation

stop, his face felt numb and he hurt all over.

Slowly, he moved his tongue around his mouth to check if his teeth were intact. They were; but when he spit, bright red blood splashed on the snow. His lips were cut badly. Absentmindedly, he felt around for his skis, which were gone. Only one pole was within reach, but when he tried to prop himself up with it, he yelped as pain went shooting through his right hand and he fell back down. He was stuck. *How am I going to get off this hill?* Just then he heard a voice calling his name, followed by a *whoosh,* and, in an instant, Pastor Mike was next to him.

"It's OK, Thomas. I'm here. Let's stand you up." Within minutes, Thomas felt strong enough to walk toward the chalet. The ski patrol met them halfway and escorted them on a snowmobile. In the first aid station, Thomas's cuts were bandaged and he had his badly sprained thumb wrapped.

When the medical staff left, Thomas sat up on the bed and apologized to Pastor Mike. "I'm so sorry. I'm such an idiot. I suppose everyone thinks this is hilarious."

Pastor Mike shook his head. "Thomas, you're not an idiot, you are a natural skier. You just let your pride get the better of you. Some of the kids laughed when you fell, but they stopped when they saw you were hurt. They've all been praying that you aren't seriously injured."

Thomas was quiet for a moment. "I still feel dumb," he said.

"We all feel that way sometimes. The best thing to do is learn from your mistakes and move on."

Thomas nodded, but hesitated when Pastor Mike motioned for them to rejoin the group. "I'm not sure I want to go out there," Thomas said.

Pastor Mike looked thoughtful. "Too bad, because I was wondering if you would be willing to help me coach some of the kids on the bunny hill." Thomas smiled and made his way back to the group. ■

> *Pride goes before destruction,*
> *and a haughty spirit before a fall.*
> —Proverbs 16:18, NKJV

Girl Who Cried "Deer"

Naomi kicked her legs up and down. "I'm bored," she moaned. The backseat of the car felt stuffy, and it made her hot and cranky.

"Why don't you read one of your books?" Mom suggested from the front seat.

"I finished them all yesterday," Naomi answered, frowning. She crossed her arms and looked over at her sister. Natalie had headphones in her ears and a thick chapter book open on her lap. *I guess I should've packed more books,* Naomi thought.

"Naomi," Dad said, "look out the window. This is your first time in Arizona. Look at how beautiful it is here!"

"OK, Dad," she sighed and looked out of the window. She didn't think that it was very exciting, though. The trees all looked the same to her.

"How much farther to the Grand Canyon, Dad?" she asked.

"We'll be there in a few hours. If

MISS BRENDA'S BEDTIME STORIES — VOLUME 1

Girl Who Cried "Deer"

you look out the window carefully," Dad added brightly, "you might see a deer!"

Natalie popped one of her headphones out of her ear. "I'm hungry. When do we get to stop for lunch?"

Mom laughed. "It's only nine thirty in the morning! Now, let's do something fun. Let's sing."

"I know," said Natalie, "let's sing 'Home, Home on the Range'!"

Naomi groaned. She really wasn't in the mood to listen to her sister sing in her big voice. But it didn't matter because her family started singing anyway! "Home, home on the range!"

Naomi pouted. Then suddenly, she had an idea. Without pausing to think about it, she shouted, "Deer!"

Everyone stopped singing and looked out of the window. "Did you see one, honey?" Dad asked.

"I think so," Naomi said slowly. "I saw his head, I think. In the trees."

"Good work!" Dad said. "Keep your eyes open, and you might see one closer up."

Naomi felt a little bad about what she did. She hadn't exactly meant to lie. It just sort of happened. *Well,* she told herself, *it's possible that I might have seen a deer's head.* Soon she almost believed it herself. So, when the family started to sing again, she blurted out, "Dad, I saw another deer!"

Dad looked. *"Hmm,"* he said. "I didn't see one. Where was it?"

Girl Who Cried "Deer"

"In the trees," she answered. "I think."

"OK," Dad answered, his voice sounding not so sure. "If you say so."

Her sister went back to her book and music, and Mom and Dad went back to talking to each other in the front seat. Naomi squirmed and looked around. She was still bored. So, again, she yelled, "Deer!"

"Naomi," Dad said, turning his head to look at her over his seat. "You need to be sure before you call *deer*!"

"Yes, Dad," Naomi answered.

Naomi tried not to holler again, but the drive was so long. Unable to resist once again, she called out excitedly, "Deer!" This time her family didn't even stop what they were doing. They ignored her! Not one of them believed that she had seen a deer.

Finally, after what seemed like forever, Dad announced, "We're here!"

Naomi bounced out of the car. She had so much fun walking around the rim of the Grand Canyon that she soon forgot all about the deer.

A few days later, they were home again, and it was time to go back to school. Naomi threw her backpack into the backseat of the car and plopped down after it. "Oh, I can't wait to see my friends," Naomi said excitedly, wiggling in her seat. She looked out the window as they drove, happily thinking about what the first day of school would be like. And that's when it happened! Up a little hill on the side of the road, right in the middle of someone's front yard, was a deer! She could hardly believe her eyes!

Naomi gasped. "Mom," she called out. "Deer!"

"Oh boy," Natalie groaned. "Here we go again!"

Girl Who Cried "Deer"

Mom didn't take her eyes off of the busy road. "There isn't a deer," she answered. "Not in the city."

"But I saw it!" Naomi insisted.

"Naomi," Mom answered. "Don't start telling stories now, OK?"

"Yes, Mom," Naomi answered, "But—"

"And no *buts*!" Mom answered.

At school, Naomi couldn't stop thinking about the deer. Maybe she had just imagined it. Maybe it wasn't there at all.

The next morning, driving to school, there it was again! Naomi didn't dare say a word. Mom and Natalie wouldn't believe her anyway. She quietly waved to the deer and smiled at it.

Each morning on the way to school, the deer was there! He was in exactly the same spot, looking down at her from the little hill. It seemed

like he was waiting just for her. Every day he stood with his pretty face turned just so she could see it as they drove by. Each day, Naomi smiled, but she didn't say a word. She had a sad, terrible feeling deep down inside because she knew why no one believed her. *Oh,* she thought, *if only I hadn't played that silly game with everyone in the car on vacation! Then they'd believe me now.*

The weekend finally arrived. Naomi brushed her hair for church and smiled at herself in the mirror. She knew what she needed to do! Everyone piled into the car for church. Naomi adjusted her seat belt so it wouldn't wrinkle her dress. Then she waited. When they were close to the spot, she said, "Mom, I know that you don't want me to talk about it, but will you please just look? Dad is driving so you can turn and look at where the deer is. Please?" She held her breath as she waited for an answer.

"Naomi," Mom sighed, "not this again." Then, with an exasperated

Girl Who Cried "Deer"

sigh, she added, "All right. I'll look."

Naomi's heart leaped with joy. They turned the corner and up on the hill, there he was! In just the same spot as every other morning. "There," Naomi pointed happily. "There it is! I told you there was a deer!"

Mom looked out the window. Naomi watched as Mom's eyes opened wide and then crinkled up as she started to laugh.

"Oh, Naomi! You did see a deer! I am going to take a guess and say that he has been here every day, hasn't he?"

"Yes," Naomi said slowly, not sure what Mom was laughing about.

"Well," Mom answered, her eyes twinkling, "he is a deer all right, but he isn't real. He is a lawn ornament! I'm happy that you were telling the truth, though."

Naomi was disappointed for a minute, but then she started to giggle too! "Well," she said, still laughing, "I did tell you the truth that I saw a deer."

Looking down at her hands, she added. "I'm sorry, everyone, that I lied to you on vacation. Will you forgive me?"

"It doesn't feel good when people don't believe you or trust you, does it?" Dad asked.

Naomi shook her head. "No, it doesn't. I don't want that to happen to me ever again!"

"We forgive you," Dad answered.

"Thanks, guys," Naomi grinned. "Hey, this reminds me of a song. 'Home, home on the range! Where the *deer* and the antelope play'!" Naomi smiled happily as her family sang along with her. ■

> *Like a madman who throws firebrands, arrows, and death, is the man who deceives his neighbor, and says, "I was only joking!"*
> —Proverbs 26:18, 19, NKJV

Mean Old Rooster

Keana loved animals. She already had Thumper. He was her big, white rabbit with long, velvety, soft ears. Thumper first belonged to Ivy, a teenage neighbor, but when Ivy got tired of feeding him and cleaning his cage, Ivy gave Thumper to Keana. Then there was Hunter, the big yellow cat who caught rats, mice, and geckos. Hunter prowled all night and slept all day on the shelf above the bag of cat food, just out of reach of Koko, Keana's chocolate-brown Labrador dog. Koko became a part of the family when Keana's parents took her to see the dogs at the animal shelter. The minute Keana saw Koko, she fell in love with her. Next, Keana got two guinea pigs, Skittles and Bugsy, a bright blue parakeet she named Ashley, and two green chameleons that kept her busy hunting live flies and bugs for them to eat.

Keana loved all her pets. And since her school was so close to her home, she often took them to class for show-and-tell.

Mean Old Rooster

But what Keana really wanted to raise were some baby chickens. "We already have a rabbit, cat, dog, guinea pigs, parakeet, and two chameleons," said Dad. "Why do we need chickens?"

"Because," replied Keana, "instead of composting our table scraps, we could feed them to the chickens, and they could lay eggs and I could gather them every morning for breakfast. Think how much money we could save. Please, Dad. We already have an old chicken coop we could clean up. And I promise I would take good care of them."

So that's how six tiny two-day-old Rhode Island Red baby chicks came to live in Keana's bathroom. At first, Keana kept them in an old ice chest that didn't have a top. She put a towel in the bottom so the chicks could keep warm. Every day she faithfully fed them, put water in the chest for them to drink, and held and cuddled each little fuzz ball. It wasn't long until the chicks grew too big for the ice chest and Keana put them into a small cage. But the most fun was when she opened the cage and they followed her around the house!

After six weeks in the house, Mom and Dad decided it was time to introduce the chicks to their new home—the chicken coop. In fact, by this time, they were no longer chicks, but had grown into pullets. (That's what you call teenage chickens.)

Every morning, without having to be reminded, Keana would put on her big rubber boots, gather up the kitchen scraps, fill a container with fresh water, and head out to the chicken coop. She would open the coop and call each of her chickens by name as they followed her back to the

Mean Old Rooster

house where she got food for Thumper and the guinea pigs. Then they would follow her to the rabbit and guinea pig cage and *cluck, cluck, cluck* as they ran around eating the seeds and grain that fell to the ground when Keana poured food into the feeding containers.

When Keana was finished, the chickens would follow her back to their coop, then Keana would look for eggs and pour out the scraps for the chickens to enjoy eating.

Each day the chickens grew bigger and bigger. One day, Keana noticed that one of the chickens, the one she had named Cherry, had grown a bigger comb on the top of her head than the others, and she was the only chicken with a couple of green tail feathers. Then early one morning, Dad thought he heard a *cock-a-doodle-doo* coming from the chicken coop. The family lived on the island of Kauai where there were lots of wild chickens running around. *Maybe,* Dad thought, *it's just a wild rooster.*

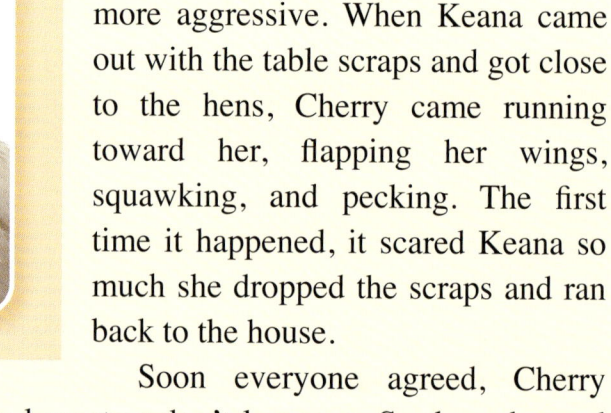

It wasn't long, however, before Cherry's comb grew bigger, her tail feathers got longer, and she became more aggressive. When Keana came out with the table scraps and got close to the hens, Cherry came running toward her, flapping her wings, squawking, and pecking. The first time it happened, it scared Keana so much she dropped the scraps and ran back to the house.

Soon everyone agreed, Cherry was a rooster, not a hen. And roosters don't lay eggs. So they changed Cherry's name to Jerry. But that didn't change his aggressive behavior. Jerry thought the five hens in the coop were his property, and he wasn't going to let anyone, not even Keana, close. So it was decided that Jerry had to go.

Since there were so many wild chickens on the island, they decided to

Mean Old Rooster

take Jerry down the mile-long dirt road and across the highway and into the forest to a little pond where lots of wild chickens lived and let Jerry have his freedom. Certainly, he would like that. He could find his own hens and have his very own family.

But Jerry had other ideas. A few days later, the children at the school Keana attended came running into the classroom, "Teacher! Teacher! There's a wild chicken outside who let us pet it and pick it up."

Keana and her friends ran outside to see. One look and Keana shouted, "That's not a wild chicken. It's Jerry!"

"Jerry? Who's Jerry?" her friends asked. "Are you talking about your mean old rooster?" Right then, Jerry strutted up to Keana and started begging for attention. Now that Jerry wasn't trying to protect his hens, he was really, really tame. Her friends gasped as Keana bent down and petted him. Jerry responded with a loud, happy, *"Cock-a-doodle-doo!"* Jerry was so tame that he let all of Keana's friends pet him.

Jerry must have thought he was a kid and belonged at school because, when recess was over and the children ran into the classroom, Jerry tagged along. When they shooed Jerry away and shut the door, Jerry found his way to the school office and flew up on the countertop and made himself at home. Then, when he heard the children coming outside and lining up for gym class, he got in line and followed them all the way to the gym.

Everyone loved Jerry. He was fun to pet, he followed the children everywhere they went, and would have even gone to chapel with them, if they would have let him. But the problem was that Jerry pooped everywhere. And no one liked chicken poop on the playground and sidewalks. Once again, it was decided that Jerry had to go.

Mean Old Rooster

This time, Elijah, a big high school kid, asked his mom if he could bring Jerry home to live with about twenty hens in their chicken coop. His mom said it was fine. So the next day, Elijah took Jerry home with him on the school bus and introduced Jerry to all the hens. Jerry didn't complain about being the only rooster in the henhouse! He was a very, very happy rooster, and he never came back to school again. And best of all, Keana could go visit Jerry at Elijah's house anytime she wanted, and Jerry never again chased, squawked, or pecked her. Jerry wasn't a mean old rooster after all.

"Jerry's not so different than some kids I know," commented Dad a few days later. "When they feel threatened or are trying to protect something, they can be mean. I guess that's why the Bible says that as much as possible we need to live peacefully with everyone including our family and friends."

"Yeah," said Keana. "When you're mean, no one wants you around; just like we tried to get ride of Jerry. But now that Jerry isn't mean anymore, everyone wants to be his friend."

> *If it is possible, as much as depends on you, live peaceably with all men.*
> —Romans 12:18, NKJV

Guilty by Association

It was the first day of school. Usually for Cameron that meant seeing all of his old friends and catching up. But not today. His family had recently moved and his new school wasn't small like his old one; it was huge! The worst part was there wasn't anyone he knew. He felt all alone.

Schedule in hand, Cameron wandered down the crowded hallway, searching for room 310 where his first class would meet. It would be different having several teachers instead of just one.

"Oops. Sorry I bumped into you." A girl with long brown hair smiled at him.

"It's OK," Cameron couldn't help but notice how pretty she was. "Hey, do you know where room 310 is?"

"I'm just heading there. First hour math. Yikes!" She was already moving, so Cameron caught up. "I'm Jenna, by the way." She ducked into a classroom door, so Cameron followed.

He stood just inside the door and looked around. Most of the seats were

MISS BRENDA'S BEDTIME STORIES — VOLUME 1

Guilty by Association

filled. The bell sounded as he stood there.

"Come on, take a seat." The person Cameron assumed was the teacher urged him forward and shut the door. Cameron found an empty seat next to Jenna and sat down. He rummaged through his backpack and retrieved a pen and notebook.

"You can't have that in here." The teacher looked right at Cameron. He didn't know what the teacher meant, so he set his pen down on his desktop.

"He means the backpack. No backpacks in class—safety first," Jenna whispered.

"Oh! I didn't know." Cameron tried to stuff the backpack under his desk, but it wouldn't fit.

"You must be new?" The teacher's eyebrows rose above his dark eyes.

Cameron just nodded, embarrassment turning his face a bright red.

"Well, remember tomorrow, OK?"

Cameron nodded again. He tried to listen as the teacher reviewed all the rules for the semester. Things were sure going to be different this year. And Cameron wasn't sure he was going to like the difference.

At lunch, Jenna and her friends took pity on Cameron and invited him to join them. Soon, lunch became a pattern, and from all appearances, Cameron had new friends. He sat with them in the morning before class and hung out with them until his mother came to pick him up. Some of the things they did and talked about bothered Cameron, such as smoking and partying. He even suspected they might be experimenting with drugs, but he wasn't sure. What he did know was that his parents wouldn't approve of the things they did! And these kids obviously weren't the kind his parents wanted him to choose as friends. But, they were friendly to him, and when he made it clear that he wasn't interested in doing those things, they didn't make fun of him or pressure him to join them.

Making friends had never been a problem in his tiny school. Everyone was a friend. So Cameron didn't know how to go about making the right

Guilty by Association

kind of friends in his new school—friends that his parents would approve of. So by default, he hung out with Jenna and her friends. When they used bad language or their talk turned to things that made him uncomfortable, he tried not to listen.

After his homework was done, Cameron sometimes texted his friends. But when they asked him to hang out with them in the park, he didn't even ask his parents if he could. He knew their rules and who they would let him hang out with. One of those rules was that before spending time with friends, Cameron was to invite them to his home so that his mom and dad could meet them. Then, and only then, could he hang out with them. And because he knew his parents would never approve of these kids, he didn't even ask. Instead, he made excuses about why he couldn't join them at the park, and pretty soon, they stopped asking.

One afternoon, when his mom came to pick him up, Cameron was excited.

"What's up? You look like you had a great day." Mom smiled as Cameron buckled his seat belt.

"I met some new guys today. They like to play football in a field near one of their homes. These are great guys, Mom. Can I go over there sometime to play with them?"

"Wait a minute. Slow down. We haven't met them yet. You know the rules."

"I'll introduce you. You'll like them, Mom. They are nice guys. They study and stay clean. Honest," Cameron pleaded.

"I can't wait to meet them." Mom pulled the car away from the school.

"Tomorrow? After school?"

Guilty by Association

"After we meet them, Dad and I will talk about it, son. But, I don't see why not."

Cameron smiled. He was truly happy for the first time since coming to this new school. He had finally found some kids to hang out with that his parents would approve of—and that he could enjoy without having to be constantly on guard.

Cameron had been right. His new friends were fun, and his parents had approved of him spending time with them. They had a blast playing football, and Cameron liked the way they talked and acted. Maybe the move wouldn't be so bad after all.

Then, suddenly, his world fell apart. Cameron had been moody all afternoon since being picked up after school. He immediately went to his room to work on his homework. His parents didn't see him until suppertime.

"Something on your mind?" His dad looked at Cameron with compassion.

"Sort of."

"What's up? You can tell us about it."

"I'm just . . . I just wish . . ."

"Wish what, son?" Mom looked concerned.

"I . . . I just wish we'd never moved." Cameron looked down at the table.

"Why?" Dad put down his fork and leaned back, looking at Cameron.

A long sigh was his only response. Finally, he looked up at his parents.

"I can't play football with the guys anymore."

"Why not? We thought you were enjoying it."

"I was, Dad. Really enjoying it. But . . . Greg plays, and, well . . . his mother is a teacher at school. She doesn't like me. So she says that Greg can't play anymore if I'm there."

Guilty by Association

"What? That doesn't make sense. We've met Mrs. Taylor. She doesn't seem unreasonable. Why would she say something like that?"

Cameron hesitated. He knew the reason; but how was he going to share it with his parents?

"It's because of my other friends."

"What friends?" Mom looked worried now.

"You know, Jenna and her gang. I've told you about them."

"But we don't let you hang around with them. I guess I don't understand."

"I hang with them at school. Mrs. Taylor thinks if I hang with them at school, I must spend time with them after school, I guess. They don't have the best reputation."

Dad pushed back from the table.

"I see. Remember when we told you that it was important to make wise choices at your new school? Just because kids come to you and want to be your friends doesn't mean that spending a lot of time with them is a wise choice."

"I know that now, Dad. Trust me. But I just can't turn my back on them. They know I don't do some of the things they do. But I don't tell on them, either. They trust me. I've encouraged them to stop doing some of the things they do, and two of them quit smoking. Someone has to show them Jesus. Right?" Cameron argued for the decision he had made.

His parents looked at him, thinking about what he had just said. Yes, someone has to show them Jesus; but was Cameron's way the best? Associating with these kids put Cameron's reputation at risk, and it could result in Cameron being pressured into joining in their bad habits. His parents had made sure Cameron didn't hang out with that particular crowd after school, but now Cameron's choice was costing him the good friends he wanted to have.

Guilty by Association

"I think we need to pray about this, son. You know, choosing good friends is like investing in your future. They will be the ones beside you when you need them. It's wise to pick friends that can do that—stand up for you and not just you standing up for them."

"So, what should I do?" Cameron asked after prayer.

"Do you think you could go and talk with Mrs. Taylor and explain the situation to her?"

"Maybe, but it doesn't seem fair that I should have to, does it?"

"Sometimes life isn't fair, Cameron. And sometimes we are guilty by association. That's why it's always wise to think things through carefully. We'll keep praying. I know God will lead you to do what is right."

The next day when Mom picked him up from school, Cameron got in the car with a big smile on his face.

"Judging from that big grin, you must have had a pretty good day," Mom said, as she shifted into gear.

"I sure did. Mom, you and Dad were right. I talked with Mrs. Taylor after school and told her everything. She was so cool—I told her how sorry I was and she thanked me for talking with her. She even invited me to their home this weekend for a barbecue she's having for Greg and his friends. Mom, I'm so sorry I wasn't honest. From now on, I'm going to choose the right friends!" ∎

> *He who walks with the wise grows wise, but a companion of fools suffers harm.*
> —Proverbs 13:20, NIV

Kristin's New Shoes

Kristin bounded toward the giant oak tree and the tire swing that hung in Grandma and Grandpa's backyard. "Come on, Boomer!" she called. "Let's play on the swing." Grandpa's obedient black Labrador charged after her, passed her up, and ran several circles around the tire swing before Kristin reached the tree. Whenever Kristin visited her grandparents, the first thing she did each day was swing. She slid her body onto the tire and began to pump. Up, down, up, down—she soared high above the huge backyard and Boomer. She closed her eyes and enjoyed the warm breeze blowing through her hair.

By the time she stopped swinging, Boomer had found a soft spot on the lawn for his morning nap. Boomer loved to sleep almost as much as Kristin loved to play on the swing.

What next? Maybe it would be fun to play house in the hay field, she thought. Her second most favorite thing to do while at her grandparents' farm was

MISS BRENDA'S BEDTIME STORIES — VOLUME 1

Kristin's New Shoes

to make a secret house in the tall hay. As she dashed past the fence to the hay field, Boomer suddenly awakened and charged after Kristin. In the middle of the field, the hay was so tall it reached Kristin's shoulders. For the next few minutes, Kristin crushed down some patches of hay. Each patch represented a room in Kristin's imaginary house.

After she and Boomer pretended to eat their supper, they went to the "bedroom" to sleep for the night. Kristin removed her shoes and stretched out on the soft mattress of hay she had prepared earlier. Boomer became her pillow. High above Kristin's head, puffy clouds drifted across the sky. The dog grunted when she pointed out a whale and a mountain lion in the billowing clouds. Sometime after she imagined a troop of elephant shapes marching across the sky, she yawned and closed her eyes.

Kristin awakened at the sound of Grandma's voice calling her name. "Kristin! Kristin!" Surprised and uncertain as to where she had fallen asleep, Kristen sat up and looked around. As she did, a drop of rain plopped on the tip of her nose.

"Oooh!" Dark storm clouds had pushed away the puffy, white elephant-shaped clouds that had been above her head when she had fallen asleep.

"Kristin!" Grandma called again from the back porch. "Kristin!"

Boomer wriggled to his feet and started running for the house, but paused at the end of the hay house to be certain Kristin would follow. After a lightning bolt snapped across the sky in the west, Kristen leaped to her feet and dashed toward the house. She and Boomer had just reached the back door as a closer lightning bolt arced between two storm clouds, followed by a loud clap of thunder.

"Here, Kristin." Grandma handed Kristin a soft, thick bath towel. "Dry yourself off while I put Boomer on the back porch and clean up the

Kristin's New Shoes

mud he's tracked in on the kitchen floor."

Grandma pointed at her granddaughter's bare feet. "Where are your shoes, honey?"

"Oh, no! I left them in the hay field! And they're brand new!" Shivering, but determined to get them, Kristin started for the back door.

"You can't go for them until the storm passes," Grandma admonished. "In the meantime, you'd better change out of your wet clothes before you get a chill."

Kristin obediently changed into a pair of her pink-flannel jammies. By the time she returned, a cup of hot cocoa was waiting for her on the kitchen table. While the rain fell and the storm winds blew, Grandma and Kristin played *Chutes and Ladders* on the living room floor in front of a roaring fire. Night fell before the storm passed. When Kristin asked Grandpa for a flashlight so she could rescue her shoes, he told her she would have to wait until morning. "It's too wet and soggy out there."

Kristin worried about her shoes as she drifted off to sleep, but there was nothing she could do about them in the middle of the night. The moment the sun came up the next morning, Kristin pulled on her blue jeans and lowered her favorite red sweatshirt down over her head. She had to find her shoes. The brisk morning air reminded her to pull the hood up over her ears. Grandma hadn't yet begun making breakfast when Kristin quietly let herself out the back door where Boomer greeted her with a delighted bark.

"*Shhhh!*" she scolded. "We have to go find my shoes." Kristin scurried across the back porch, down the steps, and across the backyard to the farm road leading to the hay field. Her toes became tiny ice

Kristin's New Shoes

cubes on the ends of her feet as she squished through the cold, soggy mud. Within a short time, she found the pathway that led to her "hay house." But her heart sank when she spied her precious shoes beside her "hay bed."

"Oh, no!" With two fingers, she held one of her new shoes up for inspection. The flower on the shoe had been chewed off. The other shoe had been chewed and then dragged several feet into what had been the "living room" of her hay house.

"Boomer! Who ate my shoes?"

The dog hung his head and whimpered.

She reached down and patted his head. "I didn't say you ate them. But some animal certainly did. Now what will I do? I know Mom doesn't have the money to buy me another pair and I can't fit into my old ones anymore. Oh, Boomer." Tears slid down her cheeks as she carried the damaged shoes back to the house.

Between sniffles Kirstin showed her grandmother the ruined shoes.

"What can I do?" she wailed. "It's not fair. Mom already spent so much money buying my backpack and my school supplies."

Grandma drew her granddaughter close and brushed a tear away that was trickling down Kristin's cheek. "Maybe we can figure out a way for you to earn money to replace your shoes."

Kristin snapped to alert. "How, Grandma?"

"Remember how I've been teaching you to make homemade bread? What if you baked a triple batch of whole wheat bread today and you sold it to people in town? They'd love the chance to buy hot-out-of-the-oven homemade bread."

Kristin's New Shoes

"Yes! I can do that. When can I start?"

Grandma laughed. "How about right now?"

Kristin dumped her ruined shoes into the garbage and hurried to the sink to wash her hands.

"Here, honey." Grandma tied a yellow and white gingham apron around Kristin's waist. "Let's get started."

Twenty loaves is a lot of bread to make, or so Kristin learned. By the time she prepared her yeast, measured and mixed the ingredients, and began kneading the dough, her muscles ached. Grandma took pity on her and helped. Kristin was thankful the bread dough needed time to rise, so she could take a little break. Grandma tried to distract her by playing a game of *Scrabble,* but every few minutes, Kristin ran into the kitchen and peered under the tea towels to be certain the dough was rising.

Once the last carefully shaped loaf of bread was in the oven, Kristin went upstairs to shower. By the time she combed out her long, brown hair, the delicious aroma of baking bread drifted up the stairwell. Her mouth watered for a bite of the freshly made bread. But she remembered her purpose. She needed the money she would get from selling the bread to buy some new shoes.

Before long, she and Grandma were in town. Grandma allowed her granddaughter to be the saleswoman for their product. Kristin sold loaves of bread to members of Grandma's church, to Grandma and Grandpa's friends, and to the grocery store owners. Everyone agreed that

Kristin's New Shoes

Kristin had done a great job baking her bread.

When all but one of the loaves had sold, Grandma agreed to buy the twentieth loaf. "Grandpa would love having freshly made bread for dinner tonight," Grandma explained. "Now it's time to drive to the mall to buy your new shoes."

In the very first shoe store, they located a pair of shoes for Kristin. She wriggled her toes inside her new shoes and grinned. The shoes exactly matched the other pair, but, for some reason, these felt extra comfortable. It must have been because she was purchasing them herself with her hard-earned money. After paying for the shoes, Kristin and Grandma drove back to the farm.

That night as Grandpa spread a thick layer of peanut butter onto a slice of Kristin's homemade bread, he asked, "So, what did you learn today?"

Kristin rolled her eyes toward the ceiling. "To take better care of my stuff."

"That's a good start. What else?" Grandpa topped the peanut butter with a thick layer of Grandma's strawberry freezer jam.

"That it's hard work to bake twenty loaves of bread."

"What else?" Grandpa asked.

After Kristin chewed a piece of bread and licked her lips, she added, "I know that I can make yummy tasting bread."

"You sure can!" Grandma exclaimed, as she cut a thick slice for herself. ∎

> *Give her the reward she has earned, and let her works bring her praise in the city gates.*
> —Proverbs 31:31, NIV

Trapped in Wildcat Cave

"**H**ey, guys," thirteen-year-old Morris Baetzold leaned across the long breakfast table at the Methodist Children's Home. "Would you like to go caving out at Wildcat Cave today?"

Billy Simpson nodded as he shoveled a spoonful of hot oatmeal into his mouth. "Yeah, let's!"

At the mere mention of caving, Billy's younger brother Sam's eyes shone. "I'll bring along my extra flashlight."

Once a year, the directors of the children's home took their charges to the Hinckley Reservation, south of Cleveland in northeastern Ohio. On numerous occasions, the three boys had hiked back into the "room" where popular legend said the local people hid runaway slaves before and during the Civil War.

On the trip to the reservation, the boys could barely conceal their excitement. Hiking down into the cave sent shivers up and down their spines,

MISS BRENDA'S BEDTIME STORIES — VOLUME 1   149

Trapped in Wildcat Cave

no matter how often they did it.

Once inside the "room," the boys tried to imagine what it must have been like for the children of the runaway slaves cowering in the darkness, waiting for word that the bounty hunters were gone so the small group of runaways could move farther north to Canada. What did they have to eat while they waited? Porridge? Corn bread? Were the children afraid of the bats that hung from the ceiling?

Sometimes during the night at the children's home, especially during an electrical storm, the boys felt terribly alone. Not having a mom or a dad whom they could turn to had drawn Morris, Billy, and Sam together. They had become inseparable friends.

After a short time exploring the nooks and cracks in the cave, Sam and Billy tired of the cave and crawled out into the sunlight.

"Hey, Morris," Billy called. "We're heading out. I think it's almost time to eat."

"OK," Morris called.

"Do you want my flashlight?" Sam asked.

"No, I'll only be a few minutes. You guys go ahead. Save me a bag lunch." One thing the boys especially liked on the outings to the reservation was the bag lunch, which always included a couple of home-made chocolate chip-cookies.

Morris peeked behind a stone slab that had fallen and blocked the crossing of the main passage. This fallen slab opened two dark triangular openings into a side passage of the cave. Curious about what might be beyond the slab, Morris slithered into the narrower of the two openings.

Trapped in Wildcat Cave

The tunnel was dark and cold. *I guess I should have taken Sam's flashlight.*

Convinced there was another room hidden farther in the mountain, he inched along in the dark. *If I find a never before discovered room, I'll be famous,* Morris thought.

Outside, the children ate their sack lunches and prepared to board the bus for home. Mr. Powell, one of the teachers, counted the children as they boarded the bus. "We're one short. Who's missing?" he asked the children on the bus.

"Where's Morris?" Billy asked. "He isn't here."

"Morris? Where did you last see him?" Mr. Powell walked along the aisle of the bus to where Sam and Billy sat.

"In Wildcat Cave. But that was before supper," Sam volunteered.

"You left him alone in the cave?" The sponsor frowned.

"Something must have happened to him. He said he'd be along any minute," Billy defended.

"OK, boys, lead me to the spot where you left him." Mr. Powell, the two boys, and three additional teachers hurried to the cave.

"Morris!" Mr. Powell shouted. "Morris!"

"Help!" From deep inside the cavern, they heard Morris' feeble reply.

"Where are you?" Mr. Powell shouted into the crack from which they had heard Morris' voice.

"I'm down here," Morris answered. "I fell through the crack."

"Can you shimmy up the wall?" Mr. Powell knelt on his knees and shined the light into the crack. Ten feet below, he could see Morris' face and head. The boy's chest and hips were wedged into a *V* of stone. In his fall, he'd toppled onto his side, trapping his right arm beneath him.

He had scratched his fingers raw with his left hand trying to get out. He couldn't reach a handhold in the rock to help pull himself up.

"No. I'm stuck. I can't move anything." Morris sounded weak and discouraged. "You'll never get me out. I'm going to die here."

When Mr. Powell stood up, Morris called, "Don't leave me. Please don't leave me."

Mr. Powell knelt down once more. "Morris, I am going to get help.

Trapped in Wildcat Cave

Billy, Sam, and Mr. Craig will stay here with you. We won't leave you alone." Mr. Craig was the boys' gym teacher at the children's home.

Mr. Powell handed Billy the flashlight. "Stay here. Keep him from panicking. I'm going to call 911."

Billy and Sam knelt down, one on each side of the crack, and shined the light down on Morris. "Don't worry, good buddy, we're here for you," Billy called.

Within minutes, firefighters and state policemen arrived. Television and newspaper reporters followed. As soon as the accident was reported on local TV and radio, volunteers came from all over the area to help rescue the boy. One viewer in particular rushed to the scene. It was Morris' dad. He hadn't seen Morris in years. After Morris' mother and father divorced, his mother died in a car crash. Then Morris' father lost track of his son.

Ideas on how to rescue the boy bounced throughout the crowd. They threw him a rope, a steel hook, and a long pole. All attempts failed.

The Cleveland Mining Company was called in to assess the situation. At first the mining engineers considered drilling their way to the boy. But upon closer study of the rock formation, they decided that the heavy drilling equipment could cause a cave-in, crushing Morris to death before they could reach him.

Hours passed. Billy and Sam hovered above the crack in the wall, trying to encourage Morris.

A trained rescue team from the National Speleological Society in Washington, D.C., flew to the site. They decided they would hook

Trapped in Wildcat Cave

mountain climbing gear to the boy and haul him out of the cave, but none of the team members were skinny enough to reach Morris and attach the equipment to him.

A five-foot two-inch nurse volunteered to try. After she slipped on a harness, the rescue workers attached a rope to it and lowered her into the hole. *Maybe this will work,* Sam thought, as he watched the nurse drop closer and closer to his trapped friend.

Two feet before she reached Morris, the nurse panicked. "No! No! Pull me out! Pull me out of here!" she wailed in terror.

The experts were frustrated. The boy had fallen within sixty feet of the mouth of the cave, yet no could get to him. Mr. Powell wrung his hands. "If only the boy had fallen with his head toward his rescuers, instead of away from them."

"If only he had both hands free, or we could get a belt on his pants," a nearby rescuer commented. "If only he'd worn clothing sturdy enough to hold a hook!"

A few miles away in Cleveland, the Ulrich family watched the drama at the cave unfold on their television.

"I'll bet one of our boys could help this kid," Andy Ulrich commented to his wife. The couple had eight sons, all strong, agile athletes.

"I don't know. With so many people there, we'd only get in the way," his wife replied.

The next morning when Andy Ulrich turned on his car radio on the way to work and learned the boy was still stuck in the cave, he decided to act. His eldest son, Michael, who was fifteen, and Gerald, who was three years younger, were small, sturdy fellows. If anyone could reach Morris, these boys could. An hour later, he and his two sons were climbing up to

Trapped in Wildcat Cave

the cave to volunteer their skills.

When Mr. Ulrich explained his plan to the professional rescuers, the experts couldn't agree on what should be done. No one wanted to send another boy into the hole for fear he might get stuck as well. Finally, when no one could come up with an alternate plan, they attached a rope to twelve-year-old Gerald and lowered him into the hole. By this time, Morris had been trapped for more than twelve hours, so the hole reeked from body odors. Gerald got to within six inches of Morris' foot and suddenly became nauseated by the strong, foul-smelling air in the cave. He gasped for air and cried to be pulled out.

Frustrated, the firemen pulled Gerald out and one of them muttered, "That's what you get for using a kid!"

"Hey, let me try," Michael Ulrich volunteered. Reluctantly, the rescue workers agreed. They tied a rope to Michael's leather belt and a nylon strap about his waist. Over his shoulder, he looped an extra rope, a strap, and a clamp, which he would attach to Morris should he reach him.

The firemen lowered Michael headfirst into the hole. Inch by inch, he dropped closer to the trapped boy. Michael talked with Morris the whole time. "Hey, buddy, I'm on my way. It's only a matter of time now, and we'll have you out of here." Finally, Michael was close enough to attach the hook to Morris. After the rescuers lifted Michael from the hole, the order was given to pull on the rope around Morris. They pulled and pulled, but the way the rope looped around the rocks, it would only move two inches.

There has to be a way, Michael reasoned. He refused to give up. Suddenly, a bright idea came to him. "How about rigging up a pulley system?"

Trapped in Wildcat Cave

The rescue team, with Michael's help, did just that; and the next time they pulled, Morris began to feel himself being lifted up, up, up.

Twenty-six-and-a-half hours after his fall—that's more than a day later—Morris took his first deep breath of fresh air, thanks to Michael's quiet, persistent courage, and the prayers of all his friends.

Morris had almost given up ever seeing his best friends again—and now Billy and Sam were hugging him, dancing around, and rejoicing. But, in addition to Billy and Sam, Morris now had a new friend for life, Michael Ulrich, who risked his life for Morris and wouldn't give up when things looked hopeless.

And the very best thing of all, because of this harrowing accident, Morris was reunited with his dad.

Michael Ulrich later received a bronze medal from the Andrew Carnegie Hero Foundation. Inscribed on the back of the bronze coin are the words "Greater love hath no man than this, that a man lay down his life for his friends." ∎

> *Greater love hath no man than this,*
> *that a man lay down his life for his friends.*
> —John 15:13, KJV

Washed Away

Kevin shivered with a chill of excitement just thinking about white water rafting. He loved water sports and just the thought of being in the middle of rushing water, hurling over the rapids, and facing unknown river currents made him tingle all over! *Maybe Tennessee isn't so bad, after all,* he thought.

Kevin and his parents had just moved east from California. The move was tough for a kid who had grown up next to the Pacific Ocean, with its crashing waves and thrill of riding the surf. The only redeeming factor was that the Ocoee (*oh-ko-ee*) River was just a short distance from their new home, and the Ocoee was one of the best white water rafting rivers in the country.

So when Chuck, Dad's friend from college, who had lived in this area most of his life, mentioned, "I've got a raft; want to go down the Ocoee?" there was no doubt in Kevin's mind—and the sooner the better.

Washed Away

At last, the big day arrived. A van was left at the end of the run, and the other vehicles gathered in the parking lot where the river rafts were launched. The shining sun, the balmy air, and the refreshing, cool water—everything was perfect for a great day on the river.

Although Chuck wasn't a professional rafting guide, he had been down the Ocoee rapids so often that he knew just exactly where the raft needed to be positioned to not flip over or get hung up on a snag.

Dad, Mom, two other friends, and Kevin strapped on their life jackets, took a paddle, and listened carefully to Chuck's instructions. "I'll be in the bow of the raft. When I yell 'Right' and point in that direction, I want you to dip your paddle deep down into the water on the right side and paddle like crazy. When I yell 'Left,' I want you to change sides and paddle on the left side like you've never paddled before. The racing water doesn't give us much time for error. I know exactly where our raft needs to be positioned to get through a rapid safely, and your paddling is what's going to get us there."

At last the group maneuvered the big rubber raft into the river, took their seats, and began paddling toward the raging water. *Whoosh,* there was no turning back now as the water grabbed the raft and hurled it toward Entrance Rapid. Everyone screamed as they were flung over the top and then dropped into the raging water below. They paddled furiously to keep exactly in the path that Chuck knew was safe. There wasn't much time between the rapids, and before Kevin knew it, they were being swept toward Gonzo Shoals, then Broken Nose.

On Second Helping, the fourth rapid, something happened, and the raft was suddenly pushed toward the rocks in the center of the river. Half of the raft went over the rocks and a jagged log—and half did not! The

Washed Away

raft balanced dangerously on huge rocks with water pounding on all sides. Chuck instructed the team to bounce up and down to see if they could get enough water under one side of the raft to lift them off the snag. It didn't work. They all moved to one side and paddled as hard as they could. That didn't work either.

"We're just too heavy," Chuck yelled above the roar of the water. "To lighten the load, I'm going to hold on to the rope around the raft, step out momentarily on those rocks and push. Then when the water lifts the raft up, I'll jump back in." It seemed like a good plan. And it almost worked.

Chuck was right. When he jumped out, the water pushed the now lighter raft off the rocks, but what no one expected was that the force of the water would rip Chuck away from the raft. Suddenly, the only person who knew anything about white-water rafting was floating down the Ocoee by himself, while the others were sitting alone in the raft.

Chuck swam over to the side of the river and grabbed hold of a tree branch that bent down into the water. Kevin and the rest of the rafters successfully paddled like mad to get the raft over to where Chuck was so they could pick him up.

Wow! Talk about adventure! By now, everyone was wet but excited about what lay ahead.

Down around Tablesaw, the raft jerked in such a way that all the rafters, except Chuck, fell out of the raft. Laughing at their mishap, they enjoyed the unexpected swim as Chuck paddled the raft to where they were. Just as Kevin and the rest were climbing back in, Chuck suddenly patted the pocket of his shorts. A worried expression crossed his face.

"Hey, Chuck," Dad called, "What's wrong?"

"My pocket's empty. I lost my wallet."

"What? You brought your wallet along on this wild ride?" Mom exclaimed.

"Yeah," said Chuck. "It has the key to my truck in it. And I had just cashed a check and I didn't want to leave all that money in the truck. I put the wallet in a plastic bag so it wouldn't get wet, but I never thought I'd lose it!"

Washed Away

"Well," Kevin said, "with all this rushing water, it's probably halfway to the Mississippi by now!"

Losing the wallet put a momentary damper on the trip. But, it was soon forgotten with the excitement of hitting Dixie Drive and Cat's Pajamas. They held on tight as Chuck maneuvered the raft through Hell Hole, then screamed for joy as the raft hit Powerhouse—the last of the rapids. It was a great run, and all too soon they were heading into shore.

"We made great time," shouted Chuck. "Paddle to that landing." It took a while to unload the raft and get into dry clothes. Chuck called home and got his wife to bring him another key to the truck.

By the time they piled into the van that would take them back to the top of the run, the Tennessee Valley River Authority had diverted the water from the Ocoee River to turbines that would generate electricity for the rest of the day.

As the loaded van headed back up the mountain, Kevin couldn't get over how different the Ocoee River looked with hardly any water in it. Since the road followed the river, Chuck began pointing out the various rapids, which were semi-dry rocks now. "That's Cat's Pajamas; there's Tablesaw; that's Double Trouble; and there's Second Helping where we got hung up on the snag—and probably where I lost my wallet."

"No way!" exclaimed Dad. "You can now walk across the whole river and hardly get your feet wet."

"The difference is amazing!" Mom shook her head.

Suddenly, Dad shouted, "Stop the car! Let's go back and look for the wallet!"

Chuck stopped the car and the whole group piled out and stood on

Washed Away

the riverbank. Chuck shook his head, "The wallet probably fell out of my pocket when I fell into the river, but there's no way it would still be here."

Kevin agreed, "With all that water, that wallet is long gone."

"You never know," said Dad. "One time, we were playing in the ocean and my friend, Gene, lost his glasses when a big wave hit him. I prayed, dove down under the water and there they were. Let's just pray and go look for the wallet. God may have a miracle in store for us, but we'll never know for sure if we don't go look."

Kevin shook his head, and thought, *It's impossible! Dad's crazy to even suggest we could find the wallet.* But he decided it was best not to say anything.

The group of rafters prayed and then split up, each heading across the Ocoee, looking for the wallet. Chuck prayed again as he started jumping from rock to rock, "Please God, help us to find my wallet!"

Immediately, the idea came to Chuck, *Look where you were holding on to the tree branch on the other side of the river.* Chuck headed in that direction. He found the branch, looked down, and noticed a corner of what looked like a plastic bag caught on a sunken log. He reached for it and pulled up the plastic bag with his completely dry wallet inside.

His shout of, "I found it!" shocked everyone.

They all shook their heads in amazement. Forming a circle right there in the riverbed, they thanked God for the incredible miracle they had just witnessed. ■

> *Ask, and it will be given to you; seek, and you will find; knock, and it will be opened to you.*
> —Matthew 7:7, NKJV